Once Upon a Parable

Once Upon a Parable

Dramas for Worship and Religious Education

by
Michael E. Moynahan, S.J.

Illustrations by
Philip G. Steele, S.J.

PAULIST PRESS
New York/Ramsey

Library of Congress
Catalog Card Number: 83-61993

ISBN: 0-8091-2586-2

Published by Paulist Press
545 Island Road, Ramsey, N.J. 07446

Printed and bound in the
United States of America

Contents

*This book is dedicated
to Leo Rock and Mario DePaoli,
two listeners
and lovers of stories*

Foreword

For over a century the parables of Jesus have provided a road marker for the changing directions of New Testament study. Adolf Jülicher's definitive break in the late nineteenth century with the predominant mode of allegorical interpretation was followed by the work of C.H. Dodd and Joachim Jeremias who saw in the parables a privileged entree to the teaching of the historical Jesus. In the 1960's a major new stage of parable study was inaugurated under the tutelage of Amos Wilder and Robert Funk. They called for appreciation of the parables as works of literature and urged the application to them of methods of literary criticism proper to other works of literature and art. Their summons was quickly heard by a generation of scholars such as Dominic Crossan and Mary Ann Tolbert, as well as Earl Breech in his recent and stimulating study, *The Silence of Jesus.* Parables are now seen not as illustrations of moral teaching or even as expressions of Jesus' instruction to his disciples or defense of his ministry before opponents, but as complex literary artifacts which invite the reader or hearer into the world of the parable where he or she may identify with the characters and hear again the open-ended challenge the parables pose to life before God. The images and dramatic structure of the parables are not husks to be discarded in order to arrive at the kernel of meaning, but a vital part of the parabolic meaning so that the medium is truly the message.

Robert Funk was aware of the need for engagement with the the images and literary dynamic of the parables when he wrote in 1966 that "interpretation of the parables should take place in parables"—a statement more honored by citation than by imitation. The dominant mode of parable study—even by Funk who has remained a leader in the area—has been through non-parabolic books and articles. Michael Moynahan's work takes up

1

Funk's challenge in an uniquely creative way. What he *does not* offer is a series of literal dramatizations of biblical stories, but the *re-presentation* of the Gospel in parables which are to be seen, heard, felt and lived. Like the Gospel parables they are often enigmatic and open-ended and like them they tease the mind into reflection on their meaning. These twelve dramatizations are the fruit of serious study, dramatic experimentation and prayer and they summon those who would use them to a similar endeavor. The study questions which follow each dramatization are carefully crafted to invite potential users to enter imaginatively into the world of the parables. As one who has seen a number of these dramatizations in a liturgical setting, I can attest to their power to communicate the good news, and as one who has taught the parables for over a decade, these parables about parables make me wonder if often I have eyes which do not see and ears which do not hear (Mark 8:14; cf. 4:10–12).

"Let the reader take note"(Mark 13:12).

John R. Donahue, S.J.
Professor of New Testament,
Jesuit School of Theology and
Graduate Theological Union, Berkeley, California

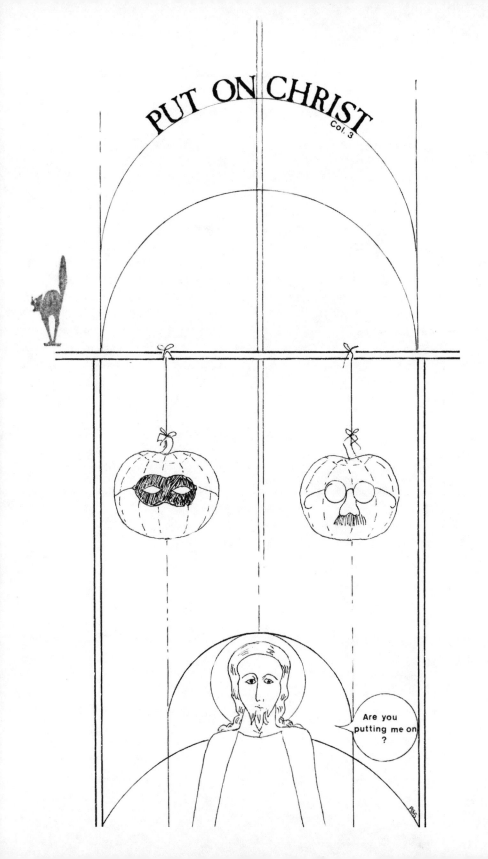

Preface

Have you ever told a story and had someone come up to you, when you were finished, and ask you: "What did it mean?" Robert Funk once wrote that the only way to interpret a parable is by telling another one.[1] Good parables, like good stories, cannot be explained. They must be experienced and entered into.

Good parables and good stories have more than one entrance and more than one exit. Part of the beauty and mystery of good narratives is that so many different people can find a home in them. To explain a story reduces points of entry and points of departure from many to one.

People of faith have a story that can be lived out and shared in many ways. Whenever we attempt to share faith we wind up telling stores. They can be stories about the time this particular person mysteriously stepped into our life and said, through words or actions or presence, precisely what we needed to hear. This person breathed new life, new faith into us. Or it might be the story about an experience that called out of us some dimension or quality of faith inside of us that we never knew existed. They can be stories of special times and special places. They can be stories of special people and experiences. They are stories that find the extraordinary buried deep within the ordinary parts of our everyday lives. They are all stories of faith.

The stories in Scripture have always held a place of importance for Christians. These stories all embody dimensions of our common journey in faith. They narrate the wonderful ways God has spoken and acted in the lives of men and women who have journeyed before us in faith. In these stories we find clues about the ways God speaks and acts in our lives today. We also find a vision of how God will be present in those parts of our journeys still to come.

Christians gather weekly to worship. Here they remember

and give thanks. Christians remember by hearing some part of the story of Scripture proclaimed again in their midst. A challenge before contemporary congregations is to find ways of allowing that Word of God to become flesh again in our here and now worship settings. The story dramatization process, developed through my work with the Berkeley Liturgical Drama Guild, is one such way.

To demonstrate this story dramatization process, I invite you to focus on the parable of the Lost Sheep. Read this parable as it is found in the fifteenth chapter of Luke's Gospel.[2] After you have read the parable, try to identify four key words or attitudes that tell the story.[3] These four words will usually be verbs. What can help you here is to remember that there are four dramatic actions that are part of any good story or drama.[4] First, there is the *initiating action*. This gets the story going. Second, there is the *developing action*. This flows out of the initiating action. Third, there is the *climaxing action*. And, finally, there is the *decisive action*. When you find these four dramatic actions in your story or parable, you will have found the four key words.

Now let's look at the parable of the Lost Sheep. What initiates the action of the story? A shepherd loses a sheep. So, the *initiating action* and first key word is *"losing."*[5] How does the action develop as a result of this loss? The shepherd seeks out the lost sheep. The *developing action* and second key word is *"seeking."* What does this seeking lead up to? It leads to the *climaxing action* and third key word which is *"finding."* And what flows out of this finding? This would be the *decisive action* and fourth key word. In this case, the decisive action is *"rejoicing."*

So the parable of the Lost Sheep is a story about losing, seeking, finding and rejoicing. John Donahue, a professor of New Testament at the Jesuit School of Theology in Berkeley, articulates a helpful distinction between exegesis and interpretation in Scripture. Exegesis is an attempt to say in my language what the Scripture is supposed to have said to its original hearers. Interpretation is an attempt to say in my language what the Scripture says to the hearers today.[6]

Exegesis and interpretation are both important. Exegesis helps guarantee faithfulness to the tradition (the original story). Interpretation invites a retelling of that story to a contemporary congregation. This retelling must be in a language a contemporary congregation understands. I believe that story drama offers us one such language. While many contemporary congregations may not be able to relate to shepherds and sheep, most, if not all, congregations can relate to experiences of losing, seeking, finding and rejoicing.

Identifying the key words of a parable or story in Scripture is the first step in the story dramatization process as we use it in the Berkeley Liturgical Drama Guild. Next, we explore the experiences locked inside of each word. Let's use the word "losing" to demonstrate this. In the Guild, we break up into groups of three or four people. We explore and share our different experiences of "losing." We can lose keys, lose contact lenses, lose children while shopping, lose directions (geographical), lose direction (psychological/spiritual), lose face, lose a friend who moves to another part of the country. We can also experience loss through death. We can lose time. We can lose heart. We can lose hope. These are just some of the experiences of losing in our lives. Each group then takes one or two of these experiences that they have shared and acts them out for the entire group This is done in silence. In other words, we mime them.

We use this technique with each of the words. After we have gone through each of the words (over a period of three weeks) we try to weave the four key words into a new story drama that speaks of the whole dynamic relationship of losing-seeking-finding-rejoicing.

Once Upon a Parable is a collection of twelve story dramatizations. Each one is based on a parable of Jesus. Each story drama utilizes the key word process that has just been described. Keep in mind that each of these story dramas is only one of the many possible creations that could come from the weaving together of that parable's four key words.

This is just one of the marvelous ways of creating an imaginative bridge between the Word of God and our own lived experience. It is a creative way of allowing the Scripture to become flesh and be proclaimed today. It is an exciting way to discover and share the mysterious depths of our Christian faith and our Christian story.

Each story drama contains a complete list of the props used

in the original production. There are also some brief notes to help those mounting productions of their own. When you use these story dramas, adapt them to your specific needs, occasions and congregations.

Each of these story dramas can be read alone for your own personal reflection and enjoyment. Each story drama can be read in a group. Different people in the group assume the various character parts. Each story drama can be fully dramatized through memorized lines and actions.

Study questions also follow each of the story dramas. They are offered as helps to those who teach. Questions and exercises are suggested to help groups break open each parable and story drama. They are not the only questions or exercises possible. Let them stir your own imaginations and shake loose other creative possibilities.

Many thanks are in order. I am grateful to John Donahue for his course on the parables of Jesus. That course helped shape each of these story dramas. I am grateful to Jake Empereur, Doug Adams, Edwina Snyder, Jack Boyle and Doyne Mraz for their suggestions and support during the course of this project. And, finally, I am grateful to all those members of the Berkeley Liturgical Drama Guild who played and prayed, who questioned and struggled, who imagined and created with me during the two and one half year gestation period of this book. *Once Upon a Parable* represents the God-gifted talents of Ray Bucko, Kevin Bradt, Mary Testin, Dan Reardon, Valerie Burns, Terese Kelly, Randy Ebelhar, Chris and Steve Kosowski, Ruth Sievert, John Coyne, John Mahedy, Theresa Kobak, Marlene Payette, John Paul, Dick Sliwinski, Martha Ann Kirk, Kathleen Tighe, Andy Utiger, Pat Curran, Mary Joe Kirt, Richard Maggi and Phil Steele.

Once Upon a Parable is a testimony to the wonderful things that come from Christians gathering around the Word of God. These story dramas are the result of people who had the courage to be vulnerable, intimate, and committed in the presence of God's Word. These story dramas were born of shared faith. Thus has it been and will it be in the history of Christianity. Whenever we come together to share faith we will wind up telling stories.

Notes

1. *Language, Hermeneutic and Word of God: The Problem of Language in the New Testament and Contemporary Theology* by Robert W. Funk. New York: Harper and Row, 1966, p. 196.

2. Luke 15:3–6.

3. I am indebted to Sr. Judith Royer of Loyola-Marymount University for both the term "key words" and a clarifying discussion of this concept that has greatly assisted me in the development of my story dramatization process.

4. My thanks to Dr. Norman Fedder of Kansas State University for his elucidation of these and his enlightening reflections on their applicability to my own work.

5. I generally put the verbs in the present participle tense.

6. "Bridging the Gap" by John R. Donahue from *Liturgical Prayer,* Vol. III, No. 3, Feb. 1973, p. 3.

1. Children and the Kingdom

(Luke 18:15–17)

They even brought babies to be touched by him. When the disciples saw this, they scolded them roundly; but Jesus called for the children, saying: "Let the little children come to me. Do not shut them off. The reign of God belongs to such as these. Trust me when I tell you that whoever does not accept the Kingdom of God as a child will not enter it."

Children and the Kingdom

Cast:

Narrator	Adult-5
Vive Ledifference	Child-1
E. Pluribus Unum	Child-2
Adult-1	Child-3
Adult-2	Child-4
Adult-3	Child-5
Adult-4	Child-V

Narrator:
Once upon a time, in a time and place very much like our own, there was a village called Harmony where two extraordinary groups of people lived. There were the adults and the children. Unlike all the other towns and villages that surrounded Harmony, the adults and children here lived in a constant spirit of peace and cooperation. Visitors were amazed to see adult and child walking hand in hand. They complemented one another perfectly. The children were continually leading the adults into wonder and discovery and the enjoyment of the now. The children would not allow any adult to forget how to play. The adults loved and treasured the children for all they gave to them. And the adults, in their turn, shared experience and knowledge and wisdom and stories with the children.

Child-1:
Hey, look at this!

Child-2:
What is it?

Adult-1:
That's what we call a mirror.

Adult-2:
Look how many amazing things you can see in it.

Child-3:
I see myself.

Adult-3:
Do you see anyone else?

Child-3:
Yeah. I see you!

Narrator:
So the children and adults played for hours in front of their newly discovered treasure. They played and explored and discovered and were delighted long into the night. But though the hour grew late and everyone was weary, the children wanted to continue. The adults, however, reminded the children that they could play tomorrow. And if any of them hoped to see tomorrow they had better rest now. And so children and adults sank into a deep and well-deserved sleep.

The next day, as the children played and the adults delighted in them, a stranger wandered into town. His name was Vive Ledifference. Vive could not believe his eyes. What were children and adults doing together?

Adult-4:
Hi, stranger! Welcome to Harmony.

Vive:
Harmony? Hummmfffppphhh!

Adult-5
What's your name, friend?

Vive:
My name is Vive Ledifference. And I am not your friend!

Adult-1:
Well, pardon the expression, stranger, but we're all friends here.

Vive:
May I be so bold as to ask why any adults in their right mind would be friends with children?

Adult-2:
Because we depend on one another here in Harmony.

Vive:
(to the adults) Well, may I speak to you for a few moments? (*The adults go to where Vive points. Vive follows. The children begin to follow Vive. Vive notices them and turns to the children.*) Alone! If you don't mind.

Narrator:
Once alone, Vive did his dastardly best to shame the adults into separating from the children

Vive:
You fools! Why are you wasting your time on these grungy urchins? What do these little pip-squeaks have to offer you? They don't have your knowledge. They don't have your experience. And they certainly don't have any of your wisdom. They take, take, take. They don't produce. They consume. They're not realistic enough. They squander all their time away in idle play. They haven't suffered enough, and so they are spoiled rotten.

Adult-1:
But they're lovable.

Vive:
Sure they're lovable when they get what they want. Say no a few times and see what happens. Spare the rod and spoil the child. Furthermore, you're all much too old to be hanging around with kids. Grow up!

Adults:
Murmur. Murmur. Murmur.

Vive:
I'll leave you alone to think about these things.

Adult-2:
What about the children?

Vive:
Leave the brats—I mean, the little dears—to me.

Narrator:
And so Vive turned and began applying his sinister charms on the children.

Vive:
Gather around me, kiddies. I have a few things to ask you.

Child-1:
Oh goodie, a game!

Child-2:
What kind of game?

Vive:
No game at all! Just zip up your lips and pay attention, all of you! What is a group of cherubic, fun-loving folks like yourselves hanging around such fuddy-duds? (*Vive points to the adults.*)

Child-1:
Because we love them!

Vive:
Sick! Sick! Sick!

Child-2:
But we feel fine!

Vive:
I mean in the head!

Child-3:
But we don't understand.

Vive:
Do you love being inhibited? Do you love having a big millstone hung around your neck? Do you love carrying around a constant admonitor all the time? Adults get tired too fast. They're more interested in logic and reason than creativity and imagination.

Child-4:
But they know so much and they're wise.

Vive:
Says who? They always say "No!" or "Tomorrow!" or "When I was your age!" The truth is that they never were your age. They were born adults. They only know how to work. They can't laugh or play. They're a drag at games. In fact, one's enough to spoil an entire party. They're so full of guilt that they're not happy until they've shared it with everybody. Just look at them grumbling over there. They're so serious. Who needs them?

Thank you all for listening to me. There are a few things I must do now. I'll see you all later.

Narrator:
With the advent of Vive Ledifference, the peace and cooperation of Harmony diminished. The adults looked at the children with critical eyes and knew fear for the first time. The children grew suspicious of the adults and they felt rejected for the first time. Only slowly and tentatively could they come back together. Just when things looked bleakest, another stranger wandered into town.

Unum:
Hello, folks!

Adult-1:
Who are you?

Unum:
My name is E. Pluribus Unum. And I've got a secret. Can I talk to you about it?

All:
Sure! (*The adults start to move one way while the children lean another way.*)

Unum:
No, no, no. Together!

Adult-1:
What is it you have to say?

Unum:
How would you all like to enter the Kingdom of God? (*The children make an outward move toward Unum.*)

Adults:
(*Each adult puts one hand over a child's eyes and another on the stomach, curtailing what the child can see and do.*) Not so fast!

Unum:
Would you like to enter the Kingdom of God? (*The children reach out toward Unum.*)

Adult-2:
What do you mean, Kingdom. That's sexist! (*Each adult puts a child's hands down.*)

Unum:
Would you like to enter the Kingdom of God? (*The children reach out toward Unum.*)

Adult-3:
What do you mean, Kingdom? This is the twentieth century. We

believe in democracy and free enterprise, not some commie kingdom! (*Adult puts child's hands down again.*)

Unum:
Would you like to enter the Kingdom of God?

Children:
(*They break free of the adults and gather around Unum.*) Yes! Yes we would!

Child-1:
Where is this Kingdom?

Unum:
Come and see! (*Here a mimed sequence begins. Unum takes the children over to the mirror. Unum walks through the mirror and the children are amazed. Then Unum, on the congregation's side of the mirror, gets the children to (1) be present to the mirror, (2) be attentive to the mirror, (3) observe what's going on in the mirror—this includes a beckoning gesture by Unum that the children imitate, (4) believe what they see and hear—this culminates in Unum extending her forefinger so it meets and touches a child's forefinger at the mirror—and (5) make a step of faith— here forefingers extend to open hands which are grasped, and Unum helps each each child walk through the mirror.*)

Narrator:
And when the children had mysteriously stepped through the mirror, the adults grew very very sad. Just when it looked as though things couldn't get any worse, Vive Ledifference returned.

Vive:
Where are the children?

Adults:
Where are the children?

Vive:
Good riddance! You won't have those pesky little rascals to bother you or distract you anymore.

Adult-1:
But life just isn't the same without them.

Unum:
Why do you all look so sad? Why aren't you happy?

Child-1:
It's just not the same without the adults. We miss them too!

Vive:
Well, where did the little monsters go?

Adult-2:
Through that. (*The adults point to the mirror.*)

Vive:
Through this? Don't be silly! This is not a door. It's a mirror. No one in one's right mind walks through mirrors. It's impossible! It simply would not make any sense at all!

Adult-3:
Well, it might not make much sense, but the children believed they could, and they did!

Vive:
What do you mean? What did they do?

Adult-1:
Well, first they were very present to the mirror. (*Adult-1 goes to the mirror area and imitates the actions of Child-1. Child-1 is now on the other side of the mirror.*)

Vive:
And then?

Adult-2:
Then they looked into the mirror and seemed to be very attentive. (*Adult-2 goes to the mirror joined on the other side of it by Child-2.*)

Vive:
And then?

Adult-3:
Then they observed what was going on in the mirror. They were open and listened. (*Adult-3 now goes to the mirror joined on the other side by Child-3.*)

Vive:
This is silly, you know, but go on. What happened next?

Adult-4:
I don't know. (*Adult-4 moves to the mirror joined on the other side by Child-4.*)

Child-4:
We believed what we saw and what we heard.

Adult-4:
They believed what they saw and what they heard.

Vive:
Believed what they saw and heard. That's ridiculous! Mirrors don't speak! Those kids were probably on some hallucinogenic drug. So what happened next?

Adult-5:
(*moving to the mirror with Child-5.*) They simply stepped through. (*This is precisely what Adult-5 does and is reunited with Child-5.*)

Vive:
They what?

Adult-1:
They stepped through. (*Here Adult-1 and Adult-3 step through the mirror and are joined again with Child-1 and Child-3.*)

Vive:
They what?

Adult-2:
They stepped through. (*Here Adult-2 and Adult-4 step through and are reunited with Child-2 and Child-4. All the adults and children make their way into the congregation now. But there is left one lonely child and Unum.*)

Vive:
This is sheer nonsense. You mean they just stepped through the mirror? Where are you? Where have you disappeared to? I know. There must be a trap door somewhere. O.K., you jokers. Come out, come out, wherever you are!

(*During the next sequence, Unum encourages the lonely child to go to the mirror and beckon Vive through. Vive winds up imitating the gestures of the child.*)

This is silly. Mirrors. Now what did they say? Oh yes, be present to the mirror. I'll give the mirror a present. How about a good swift kick in the glass? (*This action is mirrored and changed by the child.*) Then be attentive to the mirror. (*Here Vive makes a face in the mirror and then begins looking at himself.*) Then observe what's going on in the mirror. (*Here Vive does a different routine with his hands than the child does. When Vive notices this he tries to change it. Then the realization that something is happening is expressed with shocked astonishment on his face.*) Then what? Then what?

Child-V:
Believe what you see and what you hear.

Vive:
Believe what I see and hear. (*Their forefingers wind up touching, then their hands open and clasp. Both Vive and child then freeze.*)

Narrator:
Did Vive Ledifference think this was just a silly game? Some say yes, but others no. Most of the people from Harmony who were there say that Vive did believe and stepped through the mirror into that promised Kingdom. And that made the real difference, all *le difference.*

Finis

Children and the Kingdom

Theme:
Wholeness.

Props:
One large frame for a mirror. The frame is empty and large enough for the characters to easily step through it.

    Costuming can be as simple as you would like. Contrast would be helpful. You might try coordinating the adults in dark tops and light bottoms and have the children in light tops and dark bottoms. Vive Ledifference could be dressed darkly and E. Pluribus Unum lightly.

Production Notes:
It is important that the children and adults step through the mirror frame toward the congregation. The implication is that the Kingdom of God is to be found in the midst of the people of God.

Study Questions

(1) Imagine this story from Scripture in four different ways. First, become one of the people who brings a baby to Jesus. What

do you think and feel? What do you say and do? Second, become one of the disciples who scolds those people bringing babies to Jesus. What do you think and feel? What do you say and do? Third, be Jesus. What do you think and feel? What do you say and do? Fourth, be one of the babies. What do you think and feel? What do you say and do?

(2) How do children accept things? Spend some time with little children. What do you think Jesus meant when he said, "Trust me when I tell you that whoever does not accept the Kingdom of God as a child will not enter it"?

(3) Reflect on the actions of this piece of Scripture, especially: trust, accept, and enter. What experiences do these words call up in you? Consider who those people are in your life who "bring" you to Jesus. What are some of the ways Jesus "touches" you?

(4) List the best and worst qualities of adults. List the best and worst qualities of children. Who is the adult in you? Who is the child in you? Can you be whole if either the adult or the child is missing? What can the child learn from the adult? What can the adult learn from the child? How can your adult and child learn to live in harmony?

(5) Who is Vive Ledifference? What does he represent? What people, experiences or sentiments do you find divisive in your life? Look up the word prejudice in the dictionary. What does it mean? How is prejudice at work in this story drama? Discuss the prejudice, not only between children and adults, but also between different races, religions, and nations. How do you learn to make room in your mind for what other people think? How do you learn to make room in your heart for what other people feel? How do you make room in your life for people who are different from you?

(6) Have you ever been critical of someone or something? Have you ever been the object of criticism? How did you feel? What kind of criticism is helpful and what kind of criticism is harmful? List all the things you like about yourself, others and life. List all

the things you don't like about yourself, others and life. Have a conversation with God. Thank God for all that you like and experience as gift. Ask God to give you the eyes to find the gift in everything, even in what you don't like about yourself, others and life. Believe that God hears your prayer.

(7) Have you ever been fearful? List all the things, people, experiences and feelings that frighten you. Just keep asking yourself the question: "What am I afraid of?" Write down the first thing that comes to mind. Keep doing this until you can't think of anything more. Then look at your list as you listen to the song "Be Not Afraid" performed by the St. Louis Jesuits from their record album *Earthen Vessels*. [This album is produced by North American Liturgical Resources, 2110 West Peoria Avenue, Phoenix, Arizona 85029.]

(8) Who is E. Pluribus Unum? What does she represent? Why does she keep repeating the same question despite the different objections by the adults? What does the mirror represent? What must you do to pass through that mirror? What are the steps? What are the difficulties you may encounter? Do you think that Vive Ledifference stepped through the mirror? Why or why not?

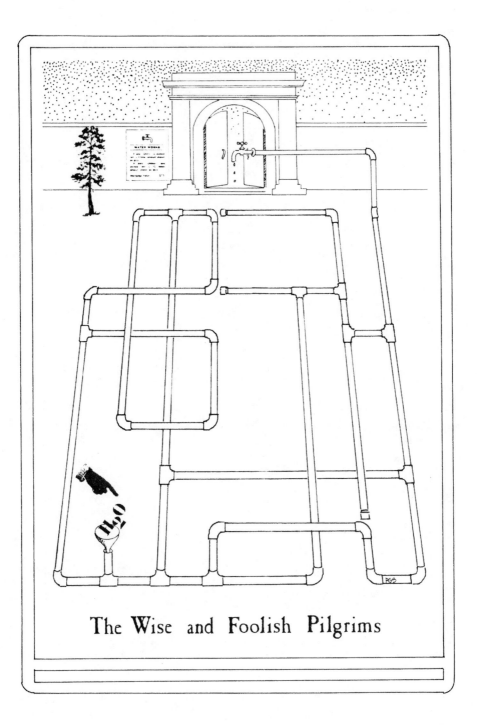

The Wise and Foolish Pilgrims

2. The Ten Bridesmaids

(Matthew 25:1–13)

"The reign of God can be likened to ten bridesmaids who took their torches and went out to welcome the groom. Five of them were wise, while the other five were foolish. The foolish ones, in taking their torches, brought no oil along, but the wise ones took flasks of oil as well as their torches. The groom delayed his coming, so they all began to nod, then to fall asleep. At midnight someone shouted, 'The groom is here! Come out and greet him!' At the outcry all the bridesmaids woke up and got their torches ready. The foolish ones said to the wise, 'Give us some of your oil. Our torches are going out.' But the wise ones replied, 'No, there may not be enough for you and us. You had better go to the dealers and buy yourselves some.' While they went off to buy it the groom arrived, and the ones who were ready went in to the wedding with him. Then the door was barred. Later the other bridesmaids came back. 'Master, master!' they cried. 'Open the door for us.' But he answered, 'I tell you, I do not know you.' The moral is: keep your eyes open, for you know not the day or the hour."

The Wise and Foolish Pilgrims

Cast:
Mother/Beggar   Tree
Older Son   Blind Person
Younger Son   Baker
Narrator   Elderly Person

Narrator:
Once upon a time there was a mother who had two children. With great satisfaction she watched her children grow. The day finally came when her children were ready to set out on their own. So she called them together and gave them a very special gift to help them on their way.

Mother:
My children, the time has come when you must leave home and search for the mysterious Kingdom of Synergy. There you will discover the secrets of life.

Younger:
Where can we find this Kingdom?

Mother:
As hard as this is to believe, my child, you will not find the Kingdom. It will find you.

Older:
And how long, may I ask, is that going to take?

Mother:
It could take a moment or a lifetime.

Older:
That's what I love, mom, precision! Think you can pinpoint it any more for us?

Mother:
I cannot help you with the time, but I do have a gift for each of you. This gift will help you in your quest.

Younger:
What is that?

Mother:
I give to each of you a container of water.

Older:
Water? I hope it didn't set you back too much!

Younger:
Will you please listen for a change and let mother finish what she has to say?

Mother:
Be very careful what you do with your water. And remember this: once you reach the Kingdom, its gates will only open to you if you sprinkle some of your water on them.

Narrator:
With that, their mother embraced them both and sent them on their way. The two young pilgrims had not traveled far before they came upon a tree.

Younger:
Look at this poor tree. See its drooping limbs? It hasn't had any water in quite some time.

Tree:
And my parched roots are thirsty. Could you give me some water?

Older:
Don't be ridiculous! Do you think it grows on trees? We only have so much. We have to be very careful how we use it. Besides, who's ever heard of a talking tree? Come on, brother, let's get out of here. (*They both start to go.*)

Tree:
Please, all I ask for is a little of your water. (*The younger brother turns and goes to the tree. He starts to pour some water around the tree when the tree speaks.*) The earth is so caked and hard around my trunk that your gift of water will do me little good unless you soften the ground by digging. Only in this way will your water reach my roots. (*The younger brother begins to dig.*)

Older:
That is simply futile! It's a waste of energy! If you do that to every tree you meet you will never get to the Kingdom. I'm leaving! (*The older brother starts off and then freezes.*)

Tree:
(*The younger brother finishes digging. He pours the water. The tree shows her relief and starts growing.*) Thank you for your kindness to me. I wish I could do something for you.

Younger:
Can you tell me how to reach the Kingdom of Synergy?

Tree:
No. But I can tell you something that may help you get there.

Younger:
What is that?

Tree:
Every creature, great or small, has something to tell you. But you must have ears to hear. And to listen, you must first be still. Some day think of the water you poured on my roots and remember that nothing is wasted.

Narrator:
The younger brother was somewhat puzzled, but thanked the tree and continued on his way. (*The younger brother turns and takes a few steps, then freezes.*) The older brother had traveled a great distance by now and came upon a blind man sitting along the roadside.

Blind:
What pilgrim passes by here?

Older:
(*Mocking*) What pilgrim passes by here? What pilgrim does it look like?

Blind:
I do not know, child, for I cannot see. Do you have any water you could spare so I can wash my tired eyes?

Older:
What good would it do? Besides, I've only got so much water and it has to last me until I get to some Kingdom called Synergy. But you just wait right here. My brother should be along any minute and he's a soft touch.

Narrator:
With that the older brother continued on his way. (*The older brother turns and takes a few steps, then freezes.*) Soon the younger brother happened upon the blind man.

Blind:
Young pilgrim, I know you have some water and that it is precious to you. Can you give this blind man a little to wash his sore eyes?

Narrator:
The younger brother could not refuse the blind man's request. So he poured some water over the blind man's eyes.

Blind:
Thank you, pilgrim. The water is refreshing. Where are you bound for?

Younger:
I'm looking for the Kingdom of Synergy. Do you know how to get there?

Blind:
Maybe "yes" and maybe "no." That's for you to judge. For I wish to tell you something that can help you on your way.

Younger:
What is that?

Blind:
Don't let your seeking blind you to your finding. Someday think of the water you gave me to cleanse my eyes and remember that nothing is wasted.

Narrator:
Still somewhat confused, the young pilgrim thanked the blind man for his advice and continued on his way. (*The younger brother turns, takes a few steps and freezes. The older brother comes to life.*) The older brother was far ahead by now and came upon a baker.

Older:
O my God! I don't believe this! First a talking tree, then a blind man and now a baker. (*The baker begins to cry.*) Correction. A crying baker! O.K., Chef Boyardee, what's the matter?

Baker:
I have no water and so I can no make a my bread. Could you give me some a water?

Older:
How is your bread going to get me any closer to my destination?

It would be a waste of my water! And I have to be careful how I
use it. Bread won't open the Kingdom's gates. It's water that I
need. (*The Baker begins to cry.*) Well, cry your little heart out.
You're not getting a drop from me!

Narrator:
And so the older brother left the baker in tears. (*Older brother
takes a few steps and freezes. The younger brother comes to life.*)
His younger brother came upon the Baker later that day.

Younger:
Baker, why are you crying?

Baker:
Because I have no water. And without water I can no bake a my
bread!

Younger:
Well, Baker, I still have plenty of water. Have some of mine.

Narrator:
Now this made the Baker very happy. He insisted that the young
pilgrim wait and take some of his freshly baked bread along for
the remainder of his journey. While the Baker worked, he and
the pilgrim talked.

Baker:
So where are you off to?

Younger:
I'm looking for the Kingdom of Synergy.

Baker:
Sounds pretty mysterious to me.

Younger:
Did you ever deliver bread there, by any chance?

Baker:
No, I'm afraid not.

Younger:
Then you couldn't tell me how to get there?

Baker:
No. But I give you something that can help you on your way.

Younger:
What is that?

Baker:
Here is your water back.

Younger:
This isn't my water. This is your bread.

Baker:
It's a both! Things change. We do not always get back exactly what we give. But your water is there in my bread. Enjoy it! Someday think of the water you gave me to bake my bread and remember that nothing is wasted.

Narrator:
The young pilgrim thanked the Baker for his wonderful bread and continued on his journey. (*The younger brother freezes. The older brother comes to life.*) The older brother was hurrying along when he noticed an elderly woman sitting by the road.

Older:
Hey, Granny, can you give me directions to the Kingdom of Synergy?

Elderly:
Can you spare a thirsty old woman a cup of water and some conversation?

Older:
Listen, Grandma, I'm tired. I'm lost. And I'm running out of water. I've got more important things to do than waste my time chatting with you.

Narrator:
So the older brother gulped some water and rushed off. (*Older brother turns and freezes. The younger brother comes to life.*) Hours later the younger brother came upon the same old woman.

Elderly:
Young man, will you give a thirsty old woman some water and conversation?

Narrator:
The younger brother felt torn. He wanted to grant both of her requests. But it was late in the day and his water was getting very low. It was when he looked into her eyes and saw her needs that his own fears were forgotten. (*Younger brother offers her some water.*)

Elderly:
Thank you, pilgrim. The water is cool and refreshing. For one so young, you seem very troubled. What ails you?

Younger:
I'm looking for the Kingdom of Synergy and I don't know if I'll ever find it.

Elderly:
Why do you seek this Kingdom?

Younger:
To discover the secrets of life and happiness.

Elderly:
Listen to an old woman who has lived many years. You do not have to go great distances to travel far. All you desire can be found in any moment, not just in a lifetime. So, be patient, pilgrim. The Kingdom you seek may be closer than you think.

Younger:
I hope so. I really do. Well, I must be on my way. Thank you for your kind words.

Elderly:
And thank you for your company. Someday think of the water and conversation you gave me and remember that nothing is wasted.

Narrator:
The young pilgrim was struck by her words. He looked long and hard at her and then nodded his assent and continued on his way. (*Younger brother freezes. The older brother comes alive.*) It was almost night and the older brother had grown desperate. He was no closer to the Kingdom than when he had started. And his water was almost gone. It was then that he came upon a beggar by the side of the road.

Beggar:
O pilgrim, have pity on me, a poor beggar! It is almost night and I am growing cold. Give me your cloak to warm myself.

Older:
And what's in it for me?

Beggar:
I have some water I would be happy to share.

Narrator:
The older brother was overjoyed. He would not run out of water now.

Older:
All right. Give me the water. (*The Beggar gives him the water. The older brother starts drinking.*)

Beggar:
(*Reaching out pleadingly, she grabs the leg of the older brother.*) And give me your cloak.

Older:
(*The older brother begins beating the Beggar. He leaves her for dead.*) That would be a waste of good clothes. And I don't think you'll be needing this anymore. (*The older brother takes the Beggar's water and starts off. Then he freezes.*)

Narrator:
Hours later the younger brother came upon the Beggar who had been left for dead. His heart went out to her in her need. He knelt down beside her and began to clean and bandage her wounds, even though it meant using the last few drops of his water. Slowly the Beggar revived.

Beggar:
Thank you, pilgrim, for your help.

Younger:
You're welcome, my friend.

Beggar:
Why do you look so sad?

Younger:
Because now I am truly lost.

Beggar:
What do you mean?

Younger:
It is night and I have not found the Kingdom of Synergy. And to make matters worse, all my water is gone. Even if I find the Kingdom, I will never be able to open its gates.

Beggar:
Since you have helped me, let me help you.

Younger:
How can you, Beggar, help me?

Beggar:
Things are not always what they seem. Do not judge by appearances. Help me up and I will show you the way to the Kingdom. You are almost there.

Narrator:
The young pilgrim helped the Beggar up. True to her word, the Beggar led the pilgrim to the Kingdom of Synergy. When they reached the gates the Beggar turned to the pilgrim.

Beggar:
Only one thing more is necessary to open these gates. Give me but one drop of water to sprinkle on them.

Younger:
But surely you must know by now that I have no water left. I have given it all away.

Tree:
He speaks the truth.

Blind:
That he does.

Baker:
He has shared it with all of us.

Elderly:
And shared himself as well.

Narrator:
The pilgrim was surprised to see all the friends he had met on his journey. It was then that the Beggar took off her rags and the young pilgrim saw his mother. He began to shed tears of gladness and joy.

Mother:
You have learned, my child, that things are not always what they seem to be. You have learned to see with your heart and not

simply judge by appearances. Do you remember how I cautioned you and your brother to be careful with the water I gave you? Do you see, now, how nothing has been wasted? (*Mother and young pilgrim embrace.*)

Younger:
But, mother, how am I to open these gates when I have no water?

Mother:
(*She puts her hands under the pilgrim's eyes and catches some tears.*) Are not these tears of joy the fruit of all you have learned? Are not these tears water? Will not this water open these gates? (*The mother sprinkles the tears on the gates and they open.*)

Narrator:
So they all went in and the gates closed behind them. There was feasting and rejoicing. Oh yes, the older brother. Word has it he was sighted somewhere in this city. He is lost and wandering to this very day.

Finis

The Wise and Foolish Pilgrims

Theme:
The Dwelling Places of God/Awareness of and Response to God's Presence in Our Lives.

Props:
(1) Two wine flasks.
(2) One little cake or loaf of bread or a large loaf that can be used later in the Eucharist.
(3) One shawl.

Study Questions

(1) Discuss what it means to be wise and what it means to be foolish. How would you define wisdom? Is the statement by a number of the characters, "Remember that nothing is wasted,"

wise or foolish? Explain. What parts of your life might this speak to? Read Matthew 25:31–46 in the light of this statement. Do you see any connection? Explain.

(2) What are the four most important images in this parable of Jesus for you? Why are they important? What do they touch in you? What is the heart of this parable for you? Do you identify with the wise or foolish people in this parable? What part of you is wise? What part of you is foolish? What type of preparation is Jesus talking about in this parable? What type of door is he talking about? What type of wisdom or foolishness is he talking about? What type of light/oil/lamp is Jesus talking about?

(3) The Tree says that every creature, great or small, has something to tell you. Do you believe this? What would be some of the things that you have heard or learned? What does it mean to have ears to hear? Is it hard to listen to? Why is it hard to listen? Why must you be still in order to listen? Read Psalm 46, verse 10. Explain what this means to you and the implications it has for your life.

(4) What did the Blind Person mean when he said, "Don't let your seeking blind you to your finding"? Have you ever experienced the truth of these words in your own life? Explain.

(5) The Baker said that things change, and that we don't always get back exactly what we give. What do you think the Baker meant? How have you experienced change in your life? How has who you were and what you have experienced contributed to making you who you are today? Do you ever stop changing or growing? Why or why not?

(6) What did the Elderly Person mean when she said "You don't have to go great distances to travel far"? How is all you desire found in any moment and not just a lifetime? What does the image/metaphor "the Kingdom of God" mean to you? You ask for the coming of this Kingdom every time you pray the Lord's Prayer. How might this Kingdom that you seek be closer than you think?

(7) The Beggar says that "things are not always what they seem." Have you experienced this as true in your own life? What does it mean to judge by appearances? What are the dangers in this? In the Gospels, how does Jesus suggest that we judge? Reflect on the following scriptural passages: Matthew 13:24–30, Matthew 12:33, and John 15:1–8. Discuss these in terms of the Beggar's advice to the Younger Brother.

(8) What does the water represent? List all the different ways it is used in this story drama. Can you think of any other uses? How does the Younger Brother open the gates of the Kingdom? Have you ever experienced tears of sadness or tears of joy? Are tears a gift from God? Why are gifts given? What do you do with gifts? How can we meet God in our feelings?

THE PEOPLE WHO DWELT ﬤ DARKNESS

3. *The Talents*

(Matthew 25:14–30)

"The case of a man who was going on a journey is similar. He called in his servants and handed his funds over to them according to each man's abilities. To one he disbursed five thousand silver pieces, to a second two thousand, and to a third a thousand. Then he went away. Immediately the man who received the five thousand went to invest it and made another five. In the same way, the man who received the two thousand doubled his figure. The man who received the thousand went off instead and dug a hole in the ground, where he buried his master's money. After a long absence, the master of those servants came home and settled accounts with them. The man who had received the five thousand came forward bringing the additional five. 'My lord,' he said, 'you let me have five thousand. See, I have made five thousand more.' His master said to him, 'Well done! You are an industrious and reliable servant. Since you were dependable in a small matter I will put you in charge of larger affairs. Come, share your master's joy!' The man who had received the two thousand then stepped forward. 'My lord,' he said, 'you entrusted me with two thousand and I have made two thousand more.' His master said to him, 'Cleverly done! You too are an industrious and reliable servant. Since you were dependable in a small matter I will put you in charge of larger affairs. Come, share your master's joy!

"Finally the man who had received the thousand stepped forward. 'My lord,' he said, 'I knew you were a hard man. You reap where you did not sow and gather where you did not scatter, so out of fear I went off and buried your thousand silver pieces in the ground. Here is your money back.' His master exclaimed: 'You worthless, lazy lout! You know I reap where I did not sow and gather where I did not scatter. All the more reason to deposit my money with the bankers, so that on my return I could have had it back with interest. You, there! Take the thousand away from him and give it to the man with the ten thousand. Those who have will get more until they grow rich, while those who have not will lose even the little they have. Throw this worthless servant into the darkness outside, where he can wail and grind his teeth.' "

The People Who Dwelt in Darkness

Cast:

Narrator	Villager-1	*(Each of these people*
Ruler	Villager-2	*play characters from*
Child	Villager-3	*the different villages.)*
	Villager-4	

Narrator:
In the middle times, between the first and second coming, there lived a kind and loving ruler. Her subjects inhabited the three villages of the realm. One day the ruler called three trusted friends together. There was one from each of the villages.

Ruler:
My friends, urgent concerns call me and my child away from the realm. In our absence I entrust the three of you with the care of our people.

Villager-3:
Well that's just great! And how are we to care for all the people?

Ruler:
I give to each of you a gift.

Villager-1:
What are they for?

Ruler:
These gifts will help you each rule wisely in our absence.

Villager-2:
We, and all your people, will anxiously await your return.

Ruler:
And we will carry remembrance of each of you in our hearts.

Narrator:
With that, the ruler and her child left on their journey. And the three trusted friends each returned with the gift to a village of the realm. (*The three villagers take the gifts of the book, the bread and wine, and the candle and move back to a zero position with the other characters.*) To the first trusted friend, the ruler gave the gift of story. He brought it back to his villagers who were all fascinated by the gift. (*Each of the villagers takes the book, examines it, and does something different with it.*)

Villager-1:
My friends, I bring you a gift from our loving ruler.

Villager-4:
What is it?

Villager-1:
It's a story.

Villager-4:
But what's a story? (*They all huddle around Villager-1. He opens the book and their heads move together up and down the pages.*)

Narrator:
The people were delighted by all they saw and heard.

All:
Ohhhhh, so that's a story.

Narrator:
An amazing thing happened. As they listened to the story their ruler had left them, it began to slowly touch and release a story in each of them.

Villager-2:
You know something, that reminds me of a story.

Villager-3:
Well, I have a story too.

Villager-4:
So do I.

Villager-1:
And I've got another one. (*Ruler and Child start leaving the group in different directions. They are sad.*)

Villager-4:
Hey, grandmother, why are you leaving?

Ruler:
I'm too old. My story is almost finished. What do I have to tell you. My story is not very exciting. It is so ordinary I'm sure it wouldn't interest you. Besides, who would want to listen to an old person's ramblings?

Villager-2:
We do!

Villager-1:
Your life has been long, your experience rich.

Villager-4:
Tell us what you have seen in life.

Villager-3:
Share with us your vision.

Narrator:
Grandmother was delighted. But as she drew a breath to begin speaking, she noticed the youngest member of the village slipping away sadly.

Ruler:
Well, what are your hopes and dreams, child? That is where you'll find your story! Why, I remember when I was your age . . .

Narrator:
Gradually the villagers learned that every person had a unique and wonderful story. And each of their stories had a special place in the story the ruler had left them.

In time the villagers learned that there were many ways to share their stories. Some sang their stories, some danced them, others painted them and still others acted them out. Some wrote their stories in prose and others in verse. Some told their stories in letters and others in song. By sharing their stories they strengthened one another in their weakness, they reassured one another when they were filled with doubts, and they comforted one another in their sadness and sorrow. Hearing even the hardest stories bolstered them and filled them all with hope. (*All the characters now return to their zero position in preparation for becoming members of the next village.*)

To the second trusted friend, the ruler gave the gift of meal. She brought the gifts of bread and wine back to her villagers who had gathered to greet her.

Villager-2:
Friends, I have brought you a gift from our loving ruler.

Villager-4:
What is it?

Villager-2:
Bread and wine.

Villager-1:
What should we do with them?

Child:
I think . . .

Villager-4:
I know. Let's save them. Let's put them away.

Child:
I think . . .

Villager-1:
I think we should put them somewhere so that the bread won't grow stale and the wine won't sour.

Child:
I think . . .

Villager-3:
No! Let's build a table. We can put the gifts on the table and gather before it every day to demonstrate our reverence and respect for them. That should make the ruler happy.

Child:
But I think we should eat and drink them.

All:
(*Shocked*) What?

Child:
What are food and drink for, after all? Let's have a meal.

Ruler:
(*Sniffing*) The child has a point, you know.

Villager-4:
They sure do smell good!

Villager-1:
They look beautiful, too.

Villager-3:
Wait a minute! Wait a minute! What if we run out?

Ruler:
How do we know we'll run out?

Villager-2:
We'll just have to take that chance.

Narrator:
And as they shared this simple meal an amazing and wonderful thing happened. As they ate and drank their eyes were opened to the many different ways they could break the bread of their lives and pour themselves out in love for one another.

They discovered that when some were hungry for someone to hear them out, others could listen and be present to them. When some were thirsty for a word that satisfied, others could speak to them from the heart. When some were hurting, naked and most vulnerable, others could touch them with healing they had experienced in their lives. When some were imprisoned, others could break through the walls dividing them and share with them in community. And when some were alone, others could offer true companionship.

Villager-2:
(*Lifting glass in a toast*) And so, friends, let's remember who has made this all possible. (*They all raise a hand in a toast. They freeze. Then they all return to the zero position in preparation to become members of the next village.*)

Narrator:
To the third trusted friend, the ruler gave the gift of light. He brought the gift back to his villagers who had awaited his return. (*He brings a big candle and a container of tapers for the villagers.*)

Villager-3:
All right, noodle-brains, quiet down!

Child:
Look at the pretty candle!

Villager-3:
Firme la bouche—if you value your life, kid! O.K., as you all know, the ruler has left the realm for some unknown reason. This gift is supposed to help us make do while she is gone—although how, I cannot figure out by any stretch of the imagination.

Villager-1:
What is it?

Ruler:
It's a light!

Villager-4:
Well, what's it for?

Ruler:
I think it's . . .

Villager-3:
I really don't think you're ready for this. Personally I am against the whole idea. But, since it was the direct wish of our ruler, I am giving each of you your own light per instructions. (*He passes out the small tapers.*)

Villager-2:
Oh, let me see yours!

Villager-4:
No, it's mine!

Villager-3:
Now don't anybody lose a candle. I am going to hold each of you personally accountable.

Child:
What are they for?

Villager-3:
Don't interrupt! I want you all to know that I am going to be held responsible for these lights. Therefore I want you to be extremely cautious and careful how you use them. Don't waste them! Get it?

All:
Got it!

Villager-3:
Good!

Child:
But what are they for?

Villager-3:
Don't be impertinent! These are a very precious commodity. And what do we do with precious commodities? (*All start to cover and hide their candles.*)

Ruler:
Share them!

Villager-3:
That's easy for you to say, grandma! You're sailing into the sunset of life! It's me who will be held responsible. Precious things must be put in their places. Therefore I decree that no one's light is to be lit. (*The child starts to light her candle from the big candle.*) And lest anyone be tempted to light a candle, I hereby order that this light be extinguished!

Narrator:
What a sad day it was for these poor villagers. Word spread to the neighboring villages about the people who dwelt in darkness.

Many years passed. Then one day the ruler returned with her child. She summoned the three friends she had entrusted with the care of her people. She was anxious to hear of them.

The first friend told the ruler of all the wonderful things the gift of story had released in his villagers. The ruler was delighted to hear of the many wonderful ways her people had learned to tell their stories.

The second friend thrilled the ruler with news of how her villagers had learned to touch one another with tenderness and compassion by sharing the meal left to them. The ruler was very, very happy.

But the ruler was stunned and saddened by the news of her third village.

Villager-3:
Here is the gift you entrusted to me.

Ruler:
But it is not lit!

Villager-3:
I was afraid that it might burn out before you returned. Then what would I have been able to give you back?

Ruler:
I gave you light and you return to me darkness. I thought you were a trusted friend. You have proven yourself a sad and foolish person. And what of my people in your village?

Villager-3:
Here are their lights.

Ruler:
All unused? All my little ones in darkness? You have not ruled wisely or with care! I can no longer trust you. (*Villager-3 begins backing away.*) And what of my poor people? What can I do for them now?

Child:
I know! I know!

Ruler:
How can I undo all the harm that has been done to them?

Child:
What about . . .

Ruler:
How can I express my care and concern?

Child:
What about sending someone . . .

Ruler:
How can I show them I have not forgotten them?

Child:
What about sending someone else to them with your gift of light?

Ruler:
But whom shall I send?

Narrator:
And after much thought, the ruler decided to send her own child to all the people who dwelt in darkness. (*The large candle is relit. The child takes a few steps in the direction of the congregation. All freeze. Then return to their original positions.*)

Finis

The People Who Dwelt in Darkness

Theme:
God's Gifts of Story, Meal and Light.

Props:
(1) One large Bible or lectionary.
(2) One large loaf of bread which can be used in the Eucharist if one follows the liturgy of the Word.
(3) One large carafe of wine which can be used in the Eucharist if one follows the liturgy of the Word.
(4) One paschal candle.
(5) Six tapers or small candles for the villagers.

Production Notes:
Because of a small cast, everyone becomes a member of each village. If you wish to employ more participants, adapt the script accordingly.

This story drama was originally done on the First Sunday of Advent. It is particularly appropriate to the Advent season.

It could be very effective to have a response to the Gospel/ homily proclamation after some moments of silent reflection. We used Dan Schutte's "Here I Am, Lord" from the St. Louis Jesuits' *Lord of Light* album in just this way.

Study Questions

(1) In the beginning of the parable, the master is very generous and gives to each person according to his or her ability. What do you understand by this? What is your ability? What do the different elements in the parable represent for you? What are the silver pieces? Do you identify with the person who received five thousand, two thousand or one thousand? Explain.

(2) What are the talents or gifts that you have been given? Reflect on this and try to write them down in your journal. What do you do with your gifts? Are there gifts that you have which you are blind to? What would it mean to increase the gifts which you have been given? Reflect on the paradox that is expressed in the Prayer of St. Francis, "It is in giving that we receive." Does this shed any light on what you can do with what you are given? Why or why not? Do you ever bury your gifts? How? Why do people bury their gifts? Why does the person who buried the thousand pieces of silver do that? Do you experience your feelings as gifts from God? Do you ever hide or bury them? Why or why not? Explain.

(3) How do you imagine God? What are your images of God? Do you think God is old, middle-aged or young? Explain. Do you think God is angry, a hard person, unfair, just, understanding or forgiving? Explain. In your journal, write down as many words as you can think of that describe who God is for you. Do you ever imagine God as a father? Do you ever imagine God as a mother? Explore some of the following images with respect to God. What would they capture about God for you? The images are: *sun, ocean, light, river, tree, rock, water, shepherd, grandparent, comedian, farmer, sculptor, musician, provider, forgiver, peacemaker, comforter, gardener, child, lover, artist, clown, friend, healer, teacher,* and *companion.* Can you think of other images that reveal some aspect of who God is for you? What would they be? Write them down in your journal and reflect on them.

(4) Read St. Paul's First Letter to the Corinthians, chapter twelve, verses four through eleven. If the Spirit distributes gifts to each person just as he chooses, what do you think the Spirit had in mind when he gave you the particular gifts you have? Explain. Often it is easier to recognize the gifts of others. Try this exercise in your family or study group. Sit in a circle. Start with one person. Have everyone in the group give thanks to God for one specific gift that he or she has experienced in this person. For example, you might pray, "I thank God for Maureen's sense of humor," or "I thank God for Maureen's loyal friendship during good times and bad times." Each person gives thanks to God for some gift in the designated person. All give thanks in their own words. When you have all thanked God for some gift in this person, then move on to the next person. Continue this way until you have done this with everyone sitting in the circle. Conclude with some final common prayer. If you know how to sing "Praise God From Whom All Blessings Flow," try that.

(5) How did the ruler relate to her people? How did the ruler's three trusted friends relate to her? Have people ever disappointed you in a relationship? How? What types of relationships realize your gifts and potential? What keeps you from being who you are? What types of relationships hide or squander your gifts or potential? How do you relate to yourself? How do you relate to others? How do you relate to your work? How do you relate to your world? How do you relate to your Church? How do you relate to God? How do each of these relationships affect you? How do your different relationships influence one another? Explain.

(6) What are the three gifts that the ruler left her people? What do they symbolize for you? What are the Scriptures a story about? Have you ever thought of yourself as a story of God? What is your favorite story from Scripture? Why is this story special to you? Grandma asks the child what her hopes and dreams are. That is where the child will find her story. What are your hopes and dreams? Reflect on this and write down your hopes and dreams in your journal. Go back to them and re-read them from time to time. How many ways do the villagers discov-

er to share their stories? Name them. Can you think of any other ways? Try sharing some part of your story in song, in dance, in painting, in drama or in some other form of expression. What happened to the villagers when they shared their stories? Can this happen to us? Discuss.

(7) What are some of the most enjoyable and memorable meals that you have ever had? Why were they so special? What do you do at meals? What are the qualities of good meals? What is missing from meals that are disappointing? Look at some of the meals recorded in Scripture. Read and reflect on: Genesis 12:1–14, Matthew 14:13–21, John 2:1–12, Mark 14:17–25, and Luke 24:13–35. What happened to the villagers when they ate the meal? What did they discover? What are some of the different ways that you can break the bread of your life and nourish other people? How have others nourished you? Explain.

(8) Why did the ruler leave her people a gift of light? Why didn't the trusted friend let the people use their lights? What was he afraid of? Has your fear of losing a gift ever prevented you from using a gift? Explain. What does it mean to be given light by someone and to return to that person darkness? What does the ruler decide to do for her people who are dwelling in darkness? Have you ever heard of Jesus referred to as the "light of the world"? What do you think this means? Read Matthew 5:14–16. What does it mean for you to be a light for the world? Reflect on this and discuss.

SMTHNG MSSNG

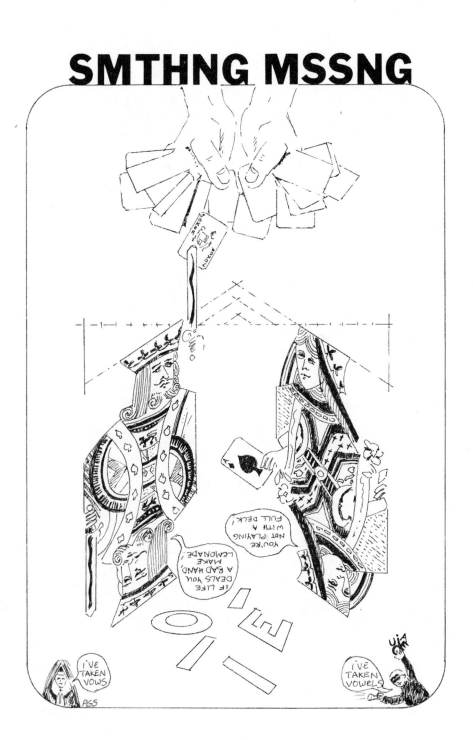

4. The Lost Coin

(Luke 15:8–10)

"What woman, if she has ten silver pieces and loses one, does not light a lamp and sweep the house in a diligent search until she has retrieved what she lost? And when she finds it, she calls in her friends and neighbors to say, 'Rejoice with me! I have found the silver piece I lost.' I tell you, there will be the same kind of joy before the angels of God over one repentant sinner."

Something Missing

Cast:

Narrator
King/Street Sweeper
Queen/Lamp Lighter
Banker
Baker
Bishop

General
Old Man
Thelma Kitch
Happy Hilda
Gotcha (A Prankster)
Bella Donna

Narrator:
Once upon a time, in the Kingdom of Come, there was a village called Harmony. The inhabitants of Harmony were different in size and shape, in color and dress, in abilities and orientations, but all somehow managed to live and work together happily— that is, until one day a messenger came with a proclamation from the King and Queen of the realm. The King and Queen decided to come to the village of Harmony and *make it (here all the villagers gasp, turn away, and generally look embarrassed and ashamed)* aaahhemmmmm . . . their home *(here the villagers sigh in relief and generally laugh and agree with the decree)*. Because of this the village began extensive preparations to ready itself for the arrival of its Royal visitors.

The Mayor had a key to the village made and worked on a welcoming speech.

Mayor:
On behalf of the villagers, I would like to welcome you, Your Royal H., and Mrs. H. And with the help of your loyal villagers we would like to extend to you a Harmony welcome. *(Here the villagers sing "Hello" four times, each time adding another part of four-part harmony.)*

Narrator:
The banker started putting all of the village's accounts in order. He estimated the costs of the preparations and had a special coin minted to commemorate the occasion. The proprietress of etiquette published the "do's" and "dont's" of living with Royalty. The Baker created pastries and recipes for banquet breads to add to the celebration. The Bishop of the village made sure that spiritual preparations were not neglected. He also composed a series of Royal blessings to mark this great event.

Bishop:
O Mars, God of War . . . no, that's a little too strong. O God whose ways are inscrutable, who seems at times to try us beyond our strength . . . no, that's too defensive. O God who strikes down the haughty and raises the lowly, bless our King and Queen. Keep them always your humble servants and through them keep us always happy. Amen.

Narrator:
The General, Otto Von Stoop, oversaw all preparations and attempted to keep the villagers busy and all things running smoothly and efficiently. However, difficulties soon developed. The banker was bothered by the Old Man of the village who simply listened to others' stories and related many of his own.

Banker:
I don't think it's fair.

Old Man:
What's not fair?

Banker:
You aren't pulling your weight!

Old Man:
You know, that reminds me of the time they had the weight pulling contest at the village fair.

Narrator:
Thelma Kitch, the proprietress of etiquette, was perturbed by the whistles and laughter that came from the most joyful member of the village, Happy Hilda.

Hilda:
Just whistle a happy tune, as you go along your way . . . (*She alternates singing the verse and whistling.*)

Thelma:
Tisk! Tisk! Hilda. One does not whistle in the presence of Royalty. Why must you insist on whistling?

Hilda:
Because I'm happy! And when I'm happy, before I know it I find myself whistling.

Thelma:
Well, if you ask me, I don't think you're taking all of our preparations seriously.

Hilda:
That's because there are so many of them that I can't keep them straight. There's preparation "A," preparation "B," preparation "C." Why there are so many preparations that if this keeps up we're all going to need preparation "H"! (*She laughs and so do some of the other villagers like the Old Man, Bella, and Gotcha.*)

Thelma:
Hmmmph!

Narrator:
The baker was concerned about Bella Donna. Bella felt the pain of others deeply. This often left her in tears. Because Bella hung around the bakery, the baker feared that her tears would destroy his pastries and bread. He also feared that her display of feelings would paralyze others and keep them from accomplishing the all-important preparations.

The General became extremely annoyed with Gotcha, the villager prankster, who interrupted and often delayed people's work.

Gotcha:
(*To the Mayor*) Pick a card, any card. All right, what is it?

Mayor:
The Queen of Hearts.

Gotcha:
You're absolutely right! (*To the Bishop*) Pick a card, any card.

Bishop:
O.K.

Gotcha:
Now pick another one. (*Leaves the Bishop confused and goes to the General.*) Pick a card, any card.

General:
(*He picks a card and Gotcha walks away.*) What am I supposed to do with this?

Gotcha:
(*Looks at congregation*) Whatever you want.

General:
But it's only one card. It's not a full deck. What use is it?

Gotcha:
Look upon it as a modest beginning. Take care of it and it might grow up to be a deck!

Narrator:
The serious and industrious members of the village resented the foolishness of certain members. Because of their repeated complaints the Mayor called a village meeting.

Mayor:
It is the feeling of many of the villagers that there are a few members of the village who are jeopardizing our preparations for the arrival of the King and Queen. Because of this, the Village Council has voted unanimously that Happy Hilda leave Harmony.

Hilda:
But why?

General:
Because one bad apple can spoil the whole bunch!

Old Man:
Well now, what if I were to tell you that Hilda is just my kind of apple?

Thelma:
I'd say "birds of a feather flock together."

Gotcha:
At least Hilda humors me and laughs at my tricks.

Banker:
She'd grab any excuse to waste her time.

Bella:
Please, don't be so mean to one another. (*Bella starts crying.*)

Baker:
Oh no! Oh no! Stop her tears! Stop her tears! She will ruin my pastries! She will drown my bread!

Mayor:
Because of the importance and nature of our preparations, I believe that it would be best for all concerned if you went your way and we went ours.

Gotcha:
Well, who needs you?

Thelma:
You took the words right out of my mouth! (*The playful villagers stick their tongues out at the serious villagers and the serious villagers raise their fists angrily at the playful ones. Hilda and the Banker go to the sign with "Harmony" written on it. They pull it apart. Hilda takes "Har" and the banker takes "Mony." Both sides turn their backs and walk away.*)

Narrator:
And so the playful members of Harmony went one way and the practical ones went another. The two camps could do what they were best at without interruption. Each was very happy for a while. The members of Har laughed and played and shared their stories with one another. Toward the end of the day, however, they grew tired and hungry. It was when they realized they had no food or shelter that Bella began to cry and all the others joined her.

The members of Mony, on the other hand, were very productive under the guidance of the General. With the "bad apples" gone, there were no distractions. Soon, however, they discovered that their work became burdensome, for there was also no laughter, no play, no joy or fun. (*All the serious villagers lower their heads sadly.*)

It was about this time that two mysterious characters arrived. A Street Sweeper stumbled upon the members of Har and a Lamp Lighter found the members of Mony. (*Both the Street Sweeper and the Lamp Lighter are dressed the same with a red clown nose on.*)

Sweeper:
Hello.

Old Man:
Howdy, stranger; what can we do for you?

Sweeper:
I thought there was a village here at one time.

Hilda:
There was but we've fallen on some hard times. Would you like to join us?

Sweeper:
I'd like to very much, but . . .

Hilda:
Why the hesitation?

Sweeper:
I can't put my finger on it, but there seems to be something missing. (*Bella starts crying.*)

Gotcha:
Pick a card, any card. (*Sweeper does.*) Well, what is it?

Sweeper:
It's just the card I want. (*Gotcha looks confused. Then all laugh.*)

Gotcha:
He's playful enough. I feel we can trust him.

Old Man:
Then welcome to Har.

Lighter:
Is this the village of Harmony?

General:
I think you are mistaken. This is now the village of Mony.

Thelma:
Who, may I ask, are you?

Lighter:
I'm a lamp lighter. I am looking for work and a place to stay.

General:
Well, we can always use someone to shed more light on what we are doing.

Banker:
Would you like to join us?

Lighter:
Thanks for the invitation. I think I would, but you know something?

Mayor:
What?

Lighter:
I can't put my finger on it, but there just seems to be something missing. (*All heads go down sadly.*)

General:
All right, cuckoos, none of that! Let's get back to work!

Narrator:
Both camps began working on the construction of shelters. The General's charges worked quickly and efficiently. The old man and his friends got lost in their stories and play. (*Both groups mime what they are doing. The one does their working while the other does their playing.*)

Sweeper:
Well, what do you think?

Old Man:
We don't have a shelter but we sure are having a good time.

Hilda:
I feel excited and happy that we are all together.

Gotcha:
I feel the rain.

Sweeper:
I think something is missing. (*Bella begins to cry.*)

Lighter:
Well, General, how do you feel about it?

General:
I think it is neat. I think it is practical. And I think it is very very ugly!

Bishop:
I think something is missing! (*All lower their heads sadly.*)

Narrator:
The next day both camps tried to bake bread in their own unique ways.

Old Man:
All right, it says here you take one cup of water. (*Gotcha takes a cup of water and hides it.*) Next, take two cups of flour. (*Hilda takes two cups and fills them with flowers.*) No! No! Not that kind of flower, the other kind!

Hilda:
Then what?

Old Man:
Knead gently. (*Everyone goes to everyone else on this.*)

Hilda:
I need you.

Gotcha:
I need you.

Bella:
I need you.

Old Man:
No! Knead gently with your hands. (*Everyone begins tickling*

everyone else and laughing.) Now wait a minute! It says knead the dough gently with your hands!

Gotcha:
Hey Hilda, what do you do when you need dough?

Hilda:
I go to the bank! (*Hilda and the rest laugh.*)

Old Man:
Speaking of needing dough, that reminds me of the depression of '29.

Sweeper:
Ahemmmm!

Old Man:
Oh yes. This just isn't working. Why don't you think it's turning out, Sweeper?

Sweeper:
Because I think there's something missing. (*Bella begins to cry.*)

Baker:
First, we need one cup of water. (*The General gives the command and it is echoed by the Bishop, the Mayor, the Banker and Thelma Kitch each time.*)

General:
One cup of water.

Baker:
Then some yeast.

General:
Yeast.

Baker:
Two cups of flour.

General:
Two cups of flour.

Baker:
Salt, sugar, cinnamon and so on.

General:
And so on.

Baker:
Knead the dough.

General:
Knead the dough.

Baker:
Bake it.

General:
Bake it. (*The General looks at his watch.*) That should do it. Well, Baker, how does it taste?

Baker:
Let's have the Lamp Lighter taste it. What do you think?

Lighter:
It's bitter. There's still something missing. (*All heads go down sadly. The Lamp Lighter lights his Light.*)

General:
What are you doing?

Lighter:
I thought I'd brighten this place up. The bread might taste a little bit better.

Banker:
It's daylight. That's impractical!

Bishop:
It might be impractical but you know what it reminds me of?

Banker:
No. What?

Bishop:
All those people who used to live with us.

Thelma:
Yes, you're right! Their stories, their feelings, their laughter and play brightened our lives.

Gotcha:
What are you doing?

Sweeper:
I thought I'd try to sweep up this mess.

Hilda:
Hey, all work and no play makes Von Stoop! (*Hilda imitates the General and all bend over with laughter.*)

Old Man:
We're laughing at him, but you know what it reminds me of?

Gotcha:
No. What?

Old Man:
General Von Stoop and all those people who used to live with us.

Gotcha:
Yeah. They knew how to get things done.

Hilda:
Their industry, their organization, their practicality kept us alive.

All:
You know, there's something missing, and it's them. (*Each group points in the direction of the other. Bella begins crying and the Baker becomes very dejected. The respective groups gather around Bella and the Baker.*)

Old Man:
Cheer up, Bella. Let's go find them! (*They all begin to look excited and happy.*)

General:
Oh, Baker, don't be sad. Cheer up and let's go find them! (*They all look excited and happy.*)

Narrator:
The Lamp Lighter pointed the way for the General and his friends. The Street Sweeper pointed the way for the Old Man and his playful companions. Slowly the members of Har and Mony made their way back to each other. When they finally found one another again there was great rejoicing. They realized how much they had missed each other. The playful villagers were dying for some food and shelter. The practical villagers entreated their friends for their songs and stories and laughter.

Gotcha:
(*To the General*) Pick a card, any card.

General:
All right, but I really think we should eat first.

Gotcha:
But I would really feel bad if you didn't pick a card. (*They show the tensions rising again.*)

Old Man:
This reminds me of how we got into this whole mess to begin with. (*Gotcha and the General look at each other, get embarrassed and laugh. The General picks a card and Gotcha takes something to eat.*)

Hilda:
Did the King and Queen ever come?

Bishop:
Not to us. We thought they might have come to you.

Gotcha:
Then they are still missing!

Baker:
They're not the only ones missing! (*Everyone looks around.*)

Hilda:
Where's the Street Sweeper?

Bishop:
Where's the Lamp Lighter? (*At this both the Street Sweeper and the Lamp Lighter come in. They are dressed the same and carry either the King and Queen puppets behind their backs or a stage prop like a crown which they can put on shortly.*)

Gotcha:
Which one is the Street Sweeper?

Banker:
And which one is the Lamp Lighter? (*They point to each other and then reveal the puppets or crowns. All the villagers gasp.*)

Thelma:
Oh no, I think I'm going to be sick.

Lighter:
Don't be frightened or ashamed, friends.

Old Man:
You came to us when we were least prepared for you.

Sweeper:
But when you needed us most.

General:
We didn't even recognize you.

Lighter:
But we knew you.

Bishop:
Why did you come to us that way?

Sweeper:
We could not come together to live with you . . .

Lighter:
. . . until you could live with yourselves. Now that Harmony is one again . . .

Sweeper:
Now that we are together and no one and nothing is missing, let the feast begin. (*They all react joyfully.*)

Narrator:
And so the feast began. The Old Man continued to bore the Baker at times. The General still got on Gotcha's nerves. But from that day forward, the villagers constantly strove to live in Harmony together.

Finis

Something Missing

Theme:
The Variety of Gifts

Props:
(1) One sign which says "HARMONY." This sign will be broken in two, so pre-cut it.

(2) One key to the city cut from cardboard and covered with gold or silver foil.

(3) One minted coin made out of a coffee can plastic top which is covered with tinfoil.

(4) One giant deck of cards which can be bought at a magic or novelty shop.

(5) One hat and apron for the Baker.

(6) Two sets of painter's overalls for the Street Sweeper and Lamp Lighter.

(7) Two clown noses for the Street Sweeper and Lamp Lighter.

(8) One long-handled broom.

(9) One candle lighter and extinguisher.

(10) Two puppets, a king and queen, or two crowns that the Street Sweeper and Lamp Lighter can bring out from behind their backs at the appropriate time.

Production Notes:

In the original performance of this story drama, done at the Pacific School of Religion in Berkeley, puppets were used for the characters of the Banker, the Bishop, Thelma Kitch and Bella Donna. Puppets are a marvelous way of enlarging your cast. With them, one person can play three characters: himself or herself, and the two puppet characters.

With the other characters in this story drama we tried to capture their personality with a hat or simple piece of clothing.

Keep in mind that necessity is the mother of invention. We used puppets because we had more characters than people in the Guild at that time. If you have more people, drop the puppets.

Study Questions

(1) Take the four key words of this parable (losing, seeking, finding and rejoicing) and do the following things with each word. First, focus on the word "losing." Think of an experience where you personally lost or where you lost something personal to you. Remember the experience and imagine it as vividly as you

can. Second, pay attention to the sequence of events (i.e., how it happened) in this experience. Third, notice the feelings you had as a result of this experience of losing. Fourth, remember the way you expressed those feelings or failed to express them. Try this with the other three key words.

(2) Using the image of the ten coins to represent a "whole," name the "ten coins" that together make up you. Have any of these parts of you been lost at different times in your life? What part of yourself might the "lost coin" represent here and now? While it is good to begin with yourself, you can also do this exercise with respect to your family, school, religious community, parish, denomination, etc.

(3) Become some object in the woman's house. You might be the light she lights or the broom she uses to sweep. You may be the "nook" or "cranny" that conceals the coin. You might even be the coin. Imagine the story unfolding. From the perspective of the object you have become, what do you think the woman is feeling? What do you observe the woman saying? What do you observe the woman doing? Reflect on all you observe and see if and how it might apply to you and your own situation.

(4) Are you more playful or practical? Would you have been with the villagers of Har or the people of Mony? Why? What do you find hard to appreciate or accept in the group of which you are not a part? What is missing in you personally? What is missing in your life? What is missing in your family? What is missing in your Church? What is missing in our world?

(5) Who are the people that gift you with stories, feelings, laughter and play? What do these gifts touch and call out of you? What is your response? How do you express your gratitude? Who are the people that gift you with their industry, organization and practicality? What do these gifts touch and call out of you? What is your response? How do you express your gratitude?

(6) Who are the Lamp Lighter and Street Sweeper? How do they help the people of Har and the people of Mony remember? How

is memory a gift in your life? In worship we remember and give thanks. Can you ever be grateful for what you cannot remember? Spend some time trying to remember important people, experiences and things in your life that you often forget or take for granted. Thank God, in your own way, for each of them. You might make it a litany of thanks. After you remember each one, say: "Thank you, God, for your great love is without end." (Based on Psalm 136.)

(7) How did the King and Queen come to the villagers of Harmony? Did the villagers recognize them? Why not? Why did the King and Queen come to the villagers in the way they did? What are some of the ways that God comes to us? Do we always recognize God? Why or why not? Why does God come to us in the ways that God does? Read Matthew's Gospel, chapter twenty-five, verses thirty-one through forty-six. Discuss it in light of these questions.

(8) What does it take to live in Harmony? What did the villagers discover that brought them together? How can their discovery or insight affect your life? Try this exercise. On a piece of paper, draw the outline of a human body. Think of all the people who influence you and help make you who you are. What part of the body would your mother and father be? Write their names on the respective part of the body. What part of the body would your brothers and sisters be? What part of the body would your neighbors and friends be? What part of the body would you be? When you have located and written in all the important people you can think of, read St. Paul's First Letter to the Corinthians, chapter twelve, verses twelve through twenty-seven.

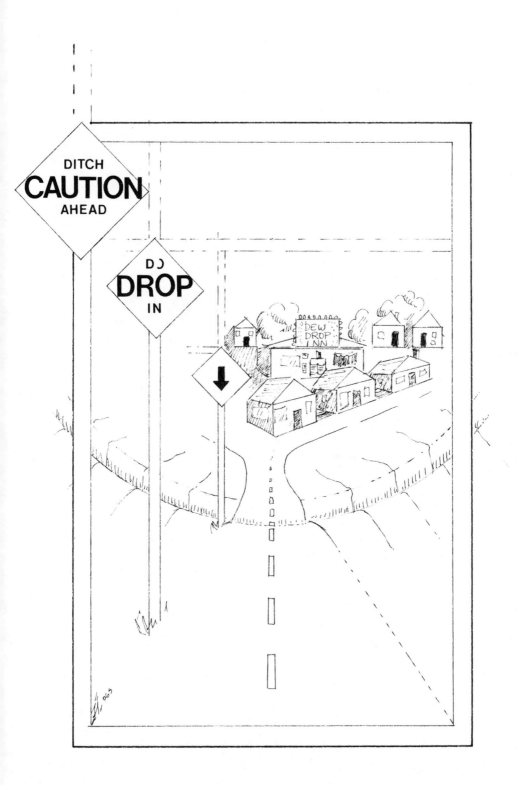

5. The Good Samaritan

(Luke 10:25–37)

On one occasion a lawyer stood up to pose him this problem: "Teacher, what must I do to inherit everlasting life?" Jesus answered him: "What is written in the law? How do you read it?" He replied:

> "You shall love the Lord your God
> with all your heart,
> with all your soul,
> with all your strength,
> and with all your mind;
> and your neighbor as yourself."

Jesus said, "You have answered correctly. Do this and you shall live." But because he wished to justify himself he said to Jesus, "And who is my neighbor?" Jesus replied: "There was a man going down from Jerusalem to Jericho who fell prey to robbers. They stripped him, beat him, and then went off leaving him half-dead. A priest happened to be going down the same road; he saw him but continued on. Likewise there was a Levite who came the same way; he saw him and went on. But a Samaritan who was journeying along came on him and was moved to pity at the sight. He approached him and dressed his wounds, pouring in oil and wine. He then hoisted him on his own beast and brought him to an inn, where he cared for him. The next day he took out two silver pieces and gave them to the innkeeper with the request: 'Look after him, and if there is any further expense I will repay you on my way back.'

"Which of these three, in your opinion, was neighbor to the man who fell in with the robbers?" The answer came, "The one who treated him with compassion." Jesus said to him, "Then go and do the same."

Do Drop In

Cast:

Narrator

Mayor

Clown

Villager-1

Villager-2

Villager-3

Villager-4

Villager-5

Villager-6

Villager-7

Villager-8

Narrator:

Once upon a time there was a village. The inhabitants of this village were happy in every respect save one. There was a ditch that completely surrounded the village. No one knew where the ditch had come from nor how long it had been there. It was a source of constant fear and anxiety for all of the villagers.

Now this ditch was unfilled and unfathomable. People who staggered dangerously near the edge of it would talk about the ditch's depth with horror. Those villagers who had relatives that fell into the ditch simply never talked about them again.

No one knew exactly how many people had fallen into the ditch. From time to time, however, they could hear the anguished cries of its inhabitants. Some said no one had ever gotten out of the ditch. Others spoke in hushed whispers of a strange shadow figure that would wander close to the ditch. And when this shadow drew near, the cries would subside for a while.

Everyone in the village was afraid of falling into the ditch. Teachers admonished students to stay on the right side of the ditch. Politicians continued to promise constituents a program of reform that would bring an end to ditches. Preachers declared the vicissitudes of wandering into dead-end ditches.

Despite all their efforts people continued to stumble into the ditch. And for those who had ears to hear, their cries were a painful reminder of the ditch's presence day and night. Finally, the people of the village called for a meeting.

Mayor:
This meeting is hereby called to order. What's our first order of business? (*Cries are heard coming from the ditch.*)

Villager-1:
That's our first order of business.

Villager-2:
We have got to do something about these cries.

Villager-3:
Those poor people are in constant agony.

Villager-4:
Funny, I don't hear anything.

Villager-5:
What can we do?

Villager-6:
Maybe someone should go down into the ditch.

Villager-7:
Don't be an idiot!

Villager-8:
Only a fool would consider getting into that mess of a ditch. (*Cries are heard again.*)

Villager-1:
Well I, for one, don't want to continue ignoring that. (*Points in the direction of the cries.*)

Villager-2:
Nor I.

Villager-3:
I agree.

Villager-5:
So do I. Their constant crying keeps me awake.

Villager-6:
Me too.

Mayor:
We don't seem to be of one mind on this subject. So, all those who believe we should do something about the noise and plight of those in the ditch please signify this by standing near the ditch. (*Villagers 1, 2, 3, 5 and 6 move near the ditch.*)
Obviously you can't live with these cries and we can. Therefore we establish you as a standing ditch committee and hereby authorize you to gather data.

Villager-8:
And what better place to gather data than in the ditch. (*The Mayor and Villagers 4, 7 and 8 push the other villagers into the ditch, then brush their hands and walk away. They will remain with backs to congregation until the end of the script when they come alive again.*)

All:
(*Cries and groans.*)

Villager-1:
Hey! You can't do that to us!

Villager-2:
Who says they can't?

Villager-5:
Well, this is another fine mess you've gotten us into.

Villager-6:
We'll just have to look at the bright side of all of this.

Villager-3:
What bright side?

Villager-6:
Well I've heard that "a ditch in time saves nine." I've also heard that "good ditches make good neighbors."

Villager-1:
I don't believe this is happening to me.

Villager-5:
You and your big mouth got us into this ditch!

Villager-6:
What ditch?

Villager-2:
Look at all this dirt.

Villager-1:
No. Don't look at the dirt. It will just get you down.

Villager-6:
Yes. Think happy thoughts. I'll bet if we all just whistle a happy tune, this will all go away. (*They attempt to whistle but begin to bump into one another.*)

Villager-2:
Owww!

Villager-3:
Hey, watch out!

Villager-1:
Will you look where you're going? (*They all begin sitting down. In the process they bump into each other.*)

Villager-5:
Leave me alone!

Villager-6:
Move over, you big lummox!

Villager-2:
What is a nice person like me doing in a pig sty like this?

Villager-3:
I hate dirt!

Villager-5:
I hate holes!

Villager-1:
I hate ditches!

All:
(*Pounding their fists against imaginary walls of ditch.*) I hate it! I hate it! Yuuuuccccckkkkk! (*After this there is a long pause. They are all exhausted and catching their breath.*)

Villager-1:
Please! Somebody! Anybody! Please let us out of here! Please! Please!

Villager-3:
What do you want from us? You want to see us grovel? Is that it? O.K., everybody, on your stomachs! Start groveling!

All:
(*On their stomachs*) Grovel! Grovel! Grovel!

Villager-3:
Now are you happy? Now will you let us out of here?

Villager-2:
If I get out of this ditch, I'll never go near another ditch as long as I live!

Villager-1:
Let us out of here and we'll never complain about ditches again!

Villager-5:
As a matter of fact, we'll never mention the dirty word again!

Villager-6:
We'll do whatever you tell us to. (*They all listen but there is no response. They sigh and look dejected.*)

Villager-2:
It's no use.

Villager-5:
There's nothing we can do.

Villager-3:
We're doomed!

Villager-6:
Well, cheer up! Things could be worse.

Villager-1:
What could be worse?

Villager-6:
It could be raining. (*There is a clap of thunder. All look up, put out hand, feel rain drop and then look at Villager-6 sternly.*)

Villager-1:
I suggest we settle in for a long, cold night.

Narrator:
And so the villagers huddled together for warmth and security. They tried to help each other be as comfortable as possible. They dried one another's tears and finally extended to each other a friendly shoulder. They tried as best they could to get some rest. (*Clown figure—i.e. a figure with a clown nose—comes near the ditch.*)

Clown:
Psst! Hello.

Villager-5:
Knock it off and go to sleep.

Clown:
Psst! Can you hear me?

Villager-2:
Yes, we can hear you! You're keeping us awake. Now we've all had a long, hard day, so just go to sleep!

Clown:
Psst! Psst!

Villager-1:
(*To Villager-6*) Will you knock that off?

Villager-6:
Will I knock what off? (*Sitting up.*)

Villager-1:
That Psst!

Villager-6:
I didn't go Psst!

Villager-1:
Then who did? (*All sit up.*)

Clown:
I did! (*They look at each other confusedly.*) Psst! Up here! (*They all look up and see the Clown.*)

Villager-1:
How did you get up there?

Clown:
I've been up here for some time.

Villager-3:
What do you want?

Clown:
I want to help you. I thought I'd just jump in the ditch and help you all.

Villager-5:
No! No! No! Stay where you are!

Villager-2:
Don't come to us! Let us come to you.

Villager-1:
If you want to help, go find a long rope and tie it to a strong tree. Or go find a tall, sturdy ladder so we can climb out of here.

Clown:
There aren't any ropes or ladders around. Anyway, who needs them? I think I could be of more help down there with you all.

Villager-6:
No! No! No! Don't jump! Please stay right where you are!

Clown:
Psst! Trust me, will you? (*The Clown jumps into the ditch.*)

All:
Ohhhh nooooo!

Villager-3:
Oh that's fine! Really fine! Now what are we going to do?

Clown:
Let's begin by having a little light on the subject. (*The Clown turns a flashlight onto his/her face revealing clearly the clown nose.*) Now follow me!

Villager-1:
What do you mean?

Clown:
Just watch me and do what I do. (*Here some miming begins. The Clown reaches out and takes someone's hand. Gradually all the villagers join hands. The Clown leads them in a circular pattern around the entire ditch. When they have stopped in front of the congregation again, the Clown takes two people. The other three villagers imitate the Clown's group. The Clown and one other villager help boost the third villager out of the ditch. The villagers out of the ditch extend a hand to the other villagers being given a boost by the Clown and other villager. Then the four villagers out of the ditch reach down in pairs and pull the Clown and remaining villager out of the ditch. When all are out there is great excitement and celebration. It is here that the Mayor and Villagers 4, 7 and 8 come to life.*)

Villager-1:
You know, that was a pretty risky and foolish thing you did for us.

Villager-2:
Why did you come down for us?

Clown:
Because you needed help and I knew I could show you the way out, if you'd let me.

Villager-3:
You mean you weren't afraid to come back into the ditch?

Clown:
Well, let me put it this way. Once you've been in the ditch, you never see anything quite the same way. (*The Clown gestures them to follow. They begin to wander off into the new world.*)

Mayor:
Wait! Wait a minute! Where are you going?

Villager-6:
There's a whole new world out here. We're going to explore it.

Villager-4:
Aren't you afraid?

Villager-5:
A little. But we can't go back.

Villager-7:
Would you let us come with you?

Villager-8:
We know we've treated you poorly but we promise to change and make it up to you.

Villager-1:
If that's what you want, then come along!

Mayor:
But we can't!

Clown:
Oh yes you can!

Villager-4:
But there's a ditch between us.

Villager-7:
We can't go around it.

Villager-8:
And we can't go over it.

Villager-1:
Then why not jump into it?

Villager-4:
How will we get out?

Villager-3:
The same way we did, with help. (*The Mayor and Villagers 4, 7 and 8 look at each other, show fear, then hold hands as they jump down into the ditch.*)

Villager-7:
I'm frightened. (*Mayor and villagers in the ditch begin moaning and crying.*)

Mayor:
We never should have done this.

Villager-8:
It's so dark down here.

Villager-4:
Get us out of here!

Mayor:
Please don't leave us here.

Villager-7:
Please. Please.

Villager-4:
Someone . . .

Villager-8:
Anyone, please help us! (*Here the villagers that are out of the ditch turn back to the ditch and bend down to look in. As they do, they conceal their putting on of clown noses. They spend some moments looking in. Then they stand up and turn to gaze at the congregation. They freeze for a moment so the congregation can see the transformation by means of the noses.*)

Mayor:
You're not going to leave us here, are you?

Villager-7:
Please. Please.

Villager-4:
Someone . . .

Villager-8:
Anyone . . .

All:
Please help us! (*The Clown and villagers who are transformed turn back to the ditch, crouch in jumping positions as the Clown had earlier, and begin the jumping movement. Then all freeze. After a few moments, all the players stand with backs to the congregation. Then all go to their places.*)
Finis

Do Drop In

Theme:
Compassion.

Props:
(1) One clown outfit which can consist of painters overalls, a colorful long sleeve T-shirt, and one red clown nose.
(2) Nine red clown noses.

Production Notes:
The ditch in this story drama must obviously be imagined. You can help your audience or congregation imagine by using a couple of street signs that warn about the "Approaching Ditch" or "Open Ditch." Another sign possibility is "Beware of Ditch."

If you do this or any of the story dramas in a church sanctuary, keep this in mind. People quickly lose interest in what they can't see. Therefore, if people can't see you when you bend down or sit down on the ground, remain standing. Adapt directorial suggestions to your respective worship spaces.

Study Questions

(1) How do you love the Lord with all your heart? How do you love the Lord with all your soul? How do you love the Lord with all your strength? How do you love the Lord with all your mind? How do you love your neighbor as yourself? Do you love yourself? Why or why not? If you love yourself poorly or not at all, can you love your neighbor any more than this? What does it mean to be a neighbor? Who are your neighbors? What is the difference between being a neighbor accidentally and purposefully?

(2) Who are the different characters in this parable? What do the different characters symbolize for you? For instance, who is the victim in you? Who are the robbers in you? What do these robbers take from you? Who is the priest in you? Who is the Levite in you? Who is the Samaritan in you? Who is the innkeeper in you? Which characters do you identify with most? Why? Explain. Which characters do you identify with least? Why? Explain. In what ways are you least like them?

(3) Choose one of the characters in the parable. Identify with that character. Don't necessarily choose a character you are comfortable with. Choose a character you want to know more about. Dialogue with that character throughout the week. What questions do you want to ask your character? Write these questions down in your journal. What replies do you imagine your character making to these questions? Write these replies down in your journal too. Reflect on what you experience and learn about your character in this way. Try this with another character in the parable.

(4) Reflect on the verbs, the actions, or this parable. What experiences, memories, associations or feelings do the words *traveling, fall prey, strip, beat, leave, see, continue on, have compassion, approach, dress, pour, lift, bring, care, give, look after,* and *repay* evoke in you? Michael Polanyi, in a book entitled

Meaning, states that we know other minds by dwelling in their acts. In this way we can get an insight into why people act the way they do. In your imagination, experience this story in three different ways. First, be the priest. Next, be the Levite. Finally, be the Samaritan. Dwell in each of their acts. Why do the priest and the Levite continue on after they see the victim? Why does the Samaritan stop?

(5) Look up the word compassion in the dictionary. What does the word mean? Literally, it means to cry out with. How does the Samaritan have compassion for the victim? Would you describe yourself as a compassionate person? Why or why not? Explain. Who are the victims in your life, in your community, in our society? What about the poor, the elderly, those who have physical or mental disabilities? What about women, the jobless, gays, the unborn? Who are some of the other victims in your life? How do you respond to them? What do you think, what do you say, what do you do in relation to them? Do you experience compassion for these groups of people? Why or why not? Explain. The priest and Levite travel by, see and pass on. The Samaritan travels by, sees and has compassion. How can what you see change your heart? What are you afraid to see in your life? Reflect on this and write your answers and reflections in your journal.

(6) What does the ditch, in the story drama, symbolize for you? Can you think of encounters or experiences you have fallen into? Imagine the cries coming from the ditch. Who are they coming from? What are the cries about? How do the villagers respond to the cries? How do you respond to the cries within you? Do you hear them? Do you pretend that they are not there? Try this exercise in your journal. Complete one of the following statements over and over again until you can't think of anything more with which to complete it. "I want _____." OR "Please help me _____." Write down the first thing that occurs to you. Reflect on all that you have written.

(7) What happens to the villagers who are pushed into the ditch? What do they experience before the Clown comes along? Elisa-

beth Kübler-Ross, in her book *On Death and Dying,* talks about the five stages people go through when they are faced with tragic news. They are: (1) denial and isolation, (2) anger, (3) bargaining, (4) depression, and (5) acceptance. Do the villagers in the ditch go through these stages? How? Discuss. We all die one physical death but are there other experiences of dying in our lives? Try to imagine and list as many experiences of figurative dying that a person can have in life. In one way or another, when you have one of these analogous experiences of death, do you go through Kübler-Ross' five stages? Why or why not? Explain.

(8) What does the Clown symbolize for you? What is the villagers' initial reaction to the Clown? How does the Clown help the villagers out of the ditch? Has the Clown been in the ditch before? Why or why not? The Clown says that once you've been in the ditch, you never see anything quite the same way. What do you think the Clown means by this? Explain. Look up the word empathy in the dictionary. What does the word mean? Is the Clown an empathetic character? How do you become an empathetic person? Do the first villagers go back to help the second group of villagers that jump into the ditch? What makes you think that they do? How are the red noses that they wear at the end of the story drama a clue to the answer? What type of unexplored world and life lie on the other side of the ditch for the villagers? Is the Clown an important part of this world and way of life? Why or why not? Explain.

MERRY LITURGIES
PRESENT

That's all, Folks!

THE CURIOUS CLUB

NOSE

6. *The Mustard Seed*

(Mark 4:30–34)

He went on to say: "What comparison shall we use for the reign of God? What image will help to present it? It is like the mustard seed which, when planted in the soil, is the smallest of all the earth's seeds, yet once it is sown, springs up to become the largest of shrubs, with branches big enough for the birds of the sky to build nests in its shade." By means of many such parables he taught them the message in a way they could understand. To them he spoke only by way of parable, while he kept explaining things privately to his disciples.

The Curious Clue

Cast:
Narrator
Mustard (A Clown)
Professor Plum
Miss Scarlet
Mrs. White
Mr. Green

Miss Peacock
Tweety Oisseau (pronounced
  Wazo)
Marcel Oisseau
Inspector Oisseau

Narrator:
Once upon a time, in the Kingdom to Come, there was a town called Ludi. The inhabitants were all musically inclined and extremely fond of whistling or humming Ludi tunes. (*Mustard, Green and Peacock hum the Looney Tunes theme. Toward the end of it, Plum, Scarlet and White hum the theme from Alfred Hitchcock.*) The best and most vocal hummers in the town were Mr. Green, a farmer; Miss Peacock, a hairdresser; and Mustard, the town clown.

Not everyone in Ludi was a hummer. There was also a small but imposing group of hoo-ers. The leader of the hoo-ers was Professor Plum, the most intelligent member of the town. He was joined by Miss Scarlet, whose chief concern was living for the moment; and Mrs. White, who felt she was on a first name basis with God, and didn't mind letting people know it.

Professor Plum and his cohorts used every occasion to impose their will on the others. But with the presence and playfulness of Mustard, this frequently became difficult or impossible. (*Here Mustard does something to get the townspeople to laugh.*)

One day two strangers appeared in town. Everyone noticed them.

111

Tweety:
(*To Professor Plum*) Hello . . .

Plum:
Goodbye! (*He leaves.*)

Tweety:
(*To Miss Scarlet*) Hello? Could you . . .

Scarlet:
Yes I could. And I'm going to! (*She joins Plum.*)

Tweety:
(*To Mrs. White*) Hello? Could you please . . .

White:
(*She puts finger to her mouth in quieting gesture.*) Shhhhhhh! (*She joins Plum and Scarlet.*)

Tweety:
This is getting us nowhere fast, Marcel. (*Marcel shows his frustration. He points to Mustard. He whistles at Mustard inaudibly. He gets Mustard's attention and gestures for him to come to them. Mustard moves toward Tweety and Marcel. Mr. Green and Miss Peacock are close behind.*)

Tweety:
Hello?

Mustard:
Hello. Who are you?

Tweety:
(*With a sigh of relief*) We're the Oisseaus. My name is Tweety and this is my brother Marcel.

Mustard:
It's nice to meet you, Tweety. How are you, Marcel? (*Marcel*

mimes everything he communicates. He mimes "tired.") I said, "How are you?" Marcel.

Tweety:
You'll have to excuse my brother, Mustard. He can't talk.

Mustard:
Well, what can I do for you?

Tweety:
Do you know the way to San Jose?

Mustard:
No, but if you hum a few bars I'll try to join in. *(Marcel laughs. Tweety gradually joins in.)* You look very tired, very hungry and very lost. *(Marcel mimes each of these out.)*

Tweety:
We are. We're looking for a place to stay. Do you think we could make our home for a while in your town?

Mustard:
That should be no problem.

Peacock:
We would love to have you.

Green:
Consider yourself at home. *(Mustard, Peacock and Green start humming "Consider Yourself" from the musical* Oliver. *Tweety and Marcel join them as they begin marching in single file. Professor Plum steps in front of the parade.)*

Plum:
Not so fast! I think you have forgotten the town ordinance that requires one of the citizens of Ludi to sponsor any visiting strangers.

Scarlet:
(*To Mr. Green*) Are you going to sponsor them, Mr. Green?

Green:
Well, no, I guess not.

White:
(*To Miss Peacock*) And you, Miss Peacock?

Peacock:
(*She looks sadly at the Oisseaus*) I'd like to, but I can't.

Mustard:
How about you, Professor Plum?

Plum:
These fly-by-nights? They're here today and gone tomorrow. There are two types of people in this world: providers and consumers. All their kind does is consume. Let me clue you in on something, Mustard. If we allow them to stay, others just like them will start flocking to our town. (*This saddens the Oisseaus.*)

Mustard:
Well then, how about Miss Scarlet.

Scarlet:
I appreciate their need. However, a little suffering is good for the stomach, as St. Paul says. It builds character. I can't really see how helping them would do anything for me. They need help. I don't. I'm O.K. and they're not. Besides, a day without adversity is like a morning without orange juice. (*The Oisseaus become sadder.*)

White:
I thoroughly agree. God helps those who help themselves. (*To the Oisseaus*) If life gives you lemons, then make Lemon Pledge. I cannot be bothered by their petty needs. I was made for greater things.

Tweety:
Can't you help us in any way?

White:
I will contribute to your spiritual welfare by sharing with you one of my famous "Range" mantras. Ommmmmmm, Ommmmmmm on the Rangeeeeeeeeee! (*The Oisseaus bow their heads and start to leave.*)

Mustard:
Where are you going?

Tweety:
There's no room for us here. (*Marcel begins to weep.*)

Mustard:
Well, I'd be happy to take you in. (*Plum, Scarlet and White look at Mustard sternly.*) I live out in the field. It wouldn't be much. But what I have, I'm willing to share with you. (*The Oisseaus smile. Marcel embraces Mustard.*)

Narrator:
As Mustard and the Oisseaus made their way to the field, Professor Plum and his cohorts were heard to murmur. (*The three of them say: "Murmur. Murmur. Murmur." Mustard and the Oisseaus go into a visual freeze as Mustard opens his umbrella-bare spokes with colored pieces of cloth attached—and the Oisseaus huddle together underneath it.*)
   During the next weeks and months, Mustard shared all he had and all he was with his new friends. The Oisseaus still met the disapproving glances of certain members of Ludi, but Mustard's care for them always seemed to be stronger. Tweety and Marcel were continually amazed by Mustard. Mustard revealed a world of mystery to them. He led them into the wonderful world of paradox. (*Mustard gives Tweety a balloon. She is pleased. Mustard then gestures to take the balloon back. Tweety protects her new-found gift. Mustard reassures her that everything is all right. She gives it to him slowly. Mustard inflates the balloon and*

returns it to her. She smiles and hugs Mustard. Mustard then goes to Marcel and hugs him. Marcel hugs Mustard back. Mustard gestures for Marcel to go to Scarlet, White and Plum. Marcel shakes his head "no." Mustard shakes his head "yes." Marcel goes to Miss Scarlet and hugs her. She pushes him away and he honks his horn playfully. Marcel tickles Mrs. White who is in her meditation position. Her hands go up in surprise and Marcel hugs her. She pushes him away and he honks his horn playfully. Next, Marcel goes to Professor Plum and hugs him. Plum pushes Marcel away and Marcel assumes a fighting pose. He looks at Mustard who shakes his head "no." Gradually Marcel relaxes and smiles and shrugs his shoulders and extends his hand to Plum. Marcel puts his bent knee in Plum's extended hand a la Harpo Marx. Then Marcel and Tweety are hugged by Mustard and join him under his umbrella which he opens. Mustard will slowly begin to go down and quietly disappear to a place of hiding. He leaves Marcel holding the umbrella.)

Professor Plum, Miss Scarlet, and Mrs. White became increasingly incensed by Mustard's actions. They determined that something had to be done. (*Here they whisper. They hum the Alfred Hitchcock theme.*)

Come the dawn, Marcel made a startling discovery. (*Marcel looks at himself holding the umbrella. He is startled.*) He quickly woke Tweety.

Tweety:
Uh? Uh? What's the matter, Marcel? (*Marcel mimes concern and urgency.*) What's wrong? (*Marcel searches his pockets looking for something.*) Something is missing? (*Marcel points to his nose.*) Your nose is missing? (*Marcel shakes his head "no." Then he motions putting some kind of spread on a piece of bread.*) Mayonnaise is missing? (*Marcel indicates "close" with his finger and then makes a bitter face.*) Mustard is missing! (*Marcel nods his assent.*) Oh my gosh, what'll we do? (*Marcel mimes the use of a spy glass.*) Right! Let's look for him.

Narrator:
They looked high and low, but there was no trace of Mustard.

Finally, they decided to go to the town square and ring the town bell to assemble the townspeople. But the bell's rope was missing. (*Marcel honks his horn and gathers the people.*)

Professor Plum and his cohorts believed they could do very well without Mustard. The others, while concerned, simply did not know which way to turn. (*Here all but Plum, Scarlet and White turn in different directions and bump into each other.*) It was Marcel who finally got an idea. (*Marcel either pulls out a lit light bulb or honks his horn to get everyone's attention.*)

Tweety:
What is it, Marcel? (*Marcel shows three fingers. He mimes his communication in a charade manner.*) Three words. First word sounds like "bend." Send! Second word. (*Marcel holds up four fingers.*) Fingers. (*Marcel shakes his head "no" and honks his horn four times.*) Four. Send for . . . Third word. Insect. Oar. Insector. Inspector! Send for our Uncle the Inspector! (*Marcel jumps up and down excitedly.*)

Narrator:
And so Tweety and Marcel sent for their world-famous Uncle, Inspector Oisseau. (*The theme from the Pink Panther plays as the Inspector makes his way to the town square. He is greeted by Tweety and Marcel.*)

Inspector:
You called? Don't tell me, there is somethin' rotten in the state of Denmark! (*Marcel shakes his head "no."*) Don't tell me. Well, perhaps you could give me a little clue. (*Marcel mimes "looking."*) You are looking for something. (*Marcel nods "yes."*) Now the question is, "What is missing?" (*Marcel mimes spreading something on a piece of bread.*) Mustard! You are missing Mustard? You fool! You mean you brought me all of this way to tell me that your mustard is missing? Go to the store and buy some more: Dijon, Poupon or French's!

Tweety:
Uncle Henry, Mustard is a clown.

Inspector:
I don't think you have recovered, my dear, from that bump on your head as a child. Mustard is a condiment.

Tweety:
But the Mustard we are looking for is a clown. And we think something terrible must have happened to him.

Inspector:
In that case, you should notify the police. (*Marcel points at the Inspector.*) That's right, Marcel, I am the police. All right, I shall personally take charge of this case.

Narrator:
Inspector Oisseau commenced interrogation of the townspeople. Soon he came to Professor Plum. (*He notices the book the Professor has and looks at it.*)

Inspector:
I shall need this for evidence. (*Plum looks shocked.*)

Narrator:
Next he questioned Miss Scarlet. (*The Inspector finds a piece of thread on Scarlet and keeps pulling and pulling it.*)

Inspector:
Terrible stuff this lint! The last time I saw lint this big was on my pet monkey!

Narrator:
Then the Inspector examined Mrs. White.

Inspector:
I seem to have run out of paper. Would you please loan me a piece of paper? (*Mrs. White gives him something to write on. Inspector looks at it and says to congregation*) An overdue notice. Very curious. (*He jots this down on the piece of paper.*) Tweety, sweetie, where was the last place that you saw Mustard alive?

Tweety:
In the field where we were sleeping.

Inspector:
Then I think we should all return to the scene of the crime.

Narrator:
Tweety led the way. As they passed by the town square, Inspector Oisseau noticed that the town bell's rope was missing. He made special note of that. (*The Inspector keeps using his magnifying glass.*)

Inspector:
Now show me exactly where he was.

Tweety:
He was right here! (*She points, looks, and sees a package. The package is a game box of "Clue."*) That's strange. I don't remember seeing this before.

Inspector:
What is it? Don't tell me. It is a box. And written on the box are the words "Do Not Open Until Found." Aha, perhaps this box is a clue, a very curious clue. Yes, it is a "Clue" box. And what is inside of this box, Marcel? (*Marcel opens the box and shows the townspeople the red noses, just like Mustard's.*) Red Noses! Red Noses? Red Noses? I suspect that there is more to these noses than meets the eye.

Tweety:
They're just like the nose that Mustard wore.

Inspector:
And what exactly did Mustard do when he wore such a nose? (*Here they all look at them nostalgically. Tweety puts one on.*)

Tweety:
He taught me that whenever I give, I really receive. (*Perhaps she has or produces a balloon as well.*)

Inspector:
And you, Marcel? (*Marcel repeats his routine with Professor Plum.*) So, he taught you how to forgive.

Narrator:
One by one, they put the red noses on and remembered the many wonderful things that Mustard had done for them and taught them. That is, everyone except Professor Plum and his two companions. This did not escape Inspector Oisseau's trained detective eye. (*Inspector jots this down.*)

Inspector:
It all adds up, Tweety, somehow. Their disdain for the red noses, the library book, the piece of lint, the overdue notice. Marcel, I know it is on the tip of my tongue. (*Marcel forces the Inspector's mouth open and looks inside.*)

Inspector:
No! No! You fool! I mean there is a thread running through all of these clues. (*Marcel points to his nose and motions "bigger."*) Bigger? Like string? (*Marcel nods "no" and repeats gesture of "bigger."*) Even bigger? (*Marcel mimes hanging himself.*) Like rope? Yes, rope! That's it, Marcel. Ladies and gentlemen, I have solved the crime.

Peacock:
Who did it, Inspector?

Green:
And where is Mustard?

Inspector:
I accuse Mrs. White (*she looks panicked*) and Miss Scarlet. (*They look at each other, terrified. They begin becoming hysterical and run to each other as they yell "No! No! No!"*)

White:
Well, if you think we are going to take this rap all by ourselves . . .

Scarlet:
You've got another think coming!

Inspector:
Silence, please! I know how to play this game. I accuse Mrs. White, Miss Scarlet *and* Professor Plum with the rope in the library! (*The crowd gasps.*) Marcel, Tweety, if I have played my cards right, you should find your friend, Mustard, tied up in the library. (*They go and bring Mustard out tied up in a rope with a gag in his mouth.*)

Narrator:
Inspector Oisseau was correct. Tweety, Marcel, Mr. Green and Miss Peacock were overjoyed to see Mustard back safe and sound. They told him the amazing story of all they had remembered when they put on the noses they then discovered he had left behind. They told him how even when they had feared he was dead, they experienced his spirit living on in them through those same noses. Finally, Inspector Oisseau interrupted them.

Inspector:
Tweety, Marcel, there are a few unresolved details which I must clear up before I go. They concern these dirty birds. (*He points to Plum, White and Scarlet.*) What do you wish to do with them? (*Marcel gestures "slit their throats."*) Give them a close shave? (*The others take their noses off, point at them and then make a sweeping gesture "to banish them."*) You want them banished? And you, Mustard, what do you want? (*Mustard goes over, gives them each a red nose and after looking at Tweety, Marcel and the others, embraces Plum, White and Scarlet.*)

Tweety:
How can you do that, Mustard, after all they have done to you?

Inspector:
Perhaps, Tweety, it is because he is a Mustard for all seasons.

Mustard:
Because no matter what they have done, they are still part of

Ludi. If we lose them, we lose parts of ourselves. Believe me, the nose knows. (*Mustard points to his clown nose. They all look at the nose in their hands and all the characters put them on. They shrug their shoulders and go to embrace Plum, White and Scarlet. Next they give Plum, White and Scarlet each a red nose. They put them on. Tweety, Marcel, Peacock and Green extend their hands in a gesture of friendship and Plum, White and Scarlet offer them their bent knees a la Harpo Marx.*)

Narrator:
All of the townspeople were amazed and delighted to discover how much Mustard's spirit had influenced them. (*They all go and pick Mustard up.*) And from that day forward they all tried to imitate Mustard's words and actions. And they all found shelter in the wisdom and shadow of Mustard the town clown. (*Here Mustard opens his umbrella once more.*)
Finis

The Curious Clue

Theme:
Hospitality

Props:
   (1) One umbrella with bare spokes and colored pieces of ribbon hanging from the spokes.
   (2) One large inflatable balloon.
   (3) One bicycle horn a la Harpo Marx.
   (4) One long piece of white cord or rope.
   (5) One book.
   (6) One long piece of white yarn.
   (7) One overdue book notice.
   (8) One "Clue" game box.
   (9) Seven red clown noses similar to the one Mustard wears.
(10) One note pad and pencil for Inspector Oisseau.

Production Notes:

Most of the characters in this story drama are patterned on characters from the detective board game "Clue." If possible, have the characters dress in the manner that their name suggests. In the original production of this story drama, Professor Plum wore a graduation hat and smoked a pipe, Miss Scarlet was dressed in red, Mrs. White wore black with a white apron, Mrs. Peacock was dressed in light blue, Mr. Green was dressed as a farmer, and Mustard wore a painter's overalls dyed yellow. Mustard also wore a red clown nose. Inspector Oisseau was dressed in a trench coat, an inspector's hat, and had a magnifying glass. Tweety and Marcel were dressed colorfully.

Study Questions

(1) Identify with one of the characters in this brief parable. Live with that character or as that character for a week and see what you can discover. Reflect and write in your journal all that you learn. What question or questions would you ask of the mustard seed if you could? What question or questions would you ask of the other characters in this parable if you could (e.g. the branches, the birds, the shade, the nests, etc.)? Listen to their replies. Reflect on them. What question or questions would the mustard seed ask of you? What question or questions would the other characters ask of you? Listen to your responses. Reflect on them.

(2) How do images affect expectations? How does what we image (imagine) affect what we see? How do expectations affect vision and experience? Jesus compared the Kingdom of God to a mustard seed. What does that image evoke imaginatively and affectively in you? What on earth do the Kingdom of God and mustard seeds have in common? Explain. What are some other images for the Kingdom of God that you can think of? Try and create some new images for the Kingdom of God. What do your images evoke imaginatively and affectively in you? Explain.

(3) Get some mustard seeds. Look at them. Touch them. Smell them. Plant them. Look up the words "annual" and "perennial" in the dictionary. What do these words mean? Is the mustard seed an annual or perennial? What are some of the implications of being an annual rather than a perennial plant? What are some of the implications of life in a nest in the shade of a shrub on the ground? Are you more vulnerable there on the ground than way up in a tree? In what ways does God call us to be vulnerable? How was Jesus vulnerable in his life? How can you become more vulnerable in your life? Is it easy? Is it important? Why or why not? Explain. How do these images and experiences teach you about the Kingdom of God as you do or don't, can or can't experience it in your own life?

(4) Make a special effort to pay attention to simple, ordinary, unspectacular, everyday parts of yourself and your life during this next week. What can you learn? Reflect on this and record what you learn in your journal. What may you have been missing? Spend some time reflecting on past experiences of your life that you expected to be great and transforming but turned out to be very disappointing. Also reflect on past experiences and encounters that you dreaded and expected nothing to come from them but which turned out to be significant and transforming experiences in your life. In your journal, on two different pages, write the word "smallest" at the top of one page and write the word "greatest" at the top of the other page. Now list all those people, experiences, things, feelings, dreams or parts of yourself that you associate with each word. Take your time. Read over the lists when you have finished. Read the parable of the Mustard Seed again. What can you learn from this? Explain and share.

(5) Who are the strangers that wander into Ludi? How do Professor Plum, Miss Scarlet and Mrs. White treat them? How do Mr. Green, Miss Peacock and Mustard treat them? Have you ever been a stranger in a new place? How did you feel? Did anyone welcome you? How did that make you feel? In Mosaic law the stranger had to be respected. Read Exodus 22:20–23. In what ways have we all been strangers at one time in our lives?

Why do you think the law defends them so strongly? Have you ever heard the phrase "A visitor comes; Christ comes"? What do you think this means? Read Matthew 25:31–40. What is hospitality? What are the ways you can be hospitable? St. Paul exhorted the Christian community at Rome to be hospitable (Romans 12:13). Imagine these words of St. Paul being addressed to you and your community. How would you respond?

(6) What does the French word *oiseau* mean? What does the phrase "That's for the birds!" mean to you? Is it a compliment or an insult? What does Mustard share with Tweety and Marcel? How does Mustard give them shelter? What does it mean to give someone shelter? What are the different ways you can literally and figuratively give shelter to another?

(7) When Inspector Oisseau solves the crime, what does Marcel suggest they do to the culprits? What do the others want to do to them? What does Mustard want to do to them? Why? What does it mean to forgive someone? Is it easy or hard to forgive? Have you ever forgiven someone for some wrong that person did to you? Has anyone ever forgiven you? How did you feel? Spend some time thinking about those people who have offended you. Remember what they did to offend you. Write down what you remember. Now see if you can forgive them. If you can, thank God for this gift. If you can't forgive them right now, ask God to give you a forgiving heart. Believe that God will hear your prayer.

(8) We reveal to others who we are by what we say and what we do. What is Professor Plum's response to the strangers? What does he say and do to them? What does this tell you about him? What is Miss Scarlet's response to the strangers? What does she say and do to them? What does this reveal to you about her? What is Mrs. White's response to the strangers? What does she say and do to them? What does this tell you about her? What is Mustard's response to the strangers? What does he say and do to them. What does this reveal to you about him? Which of these four characters do you identify with? Why? Explain. Which character would you like to imitate? Why? Explain.

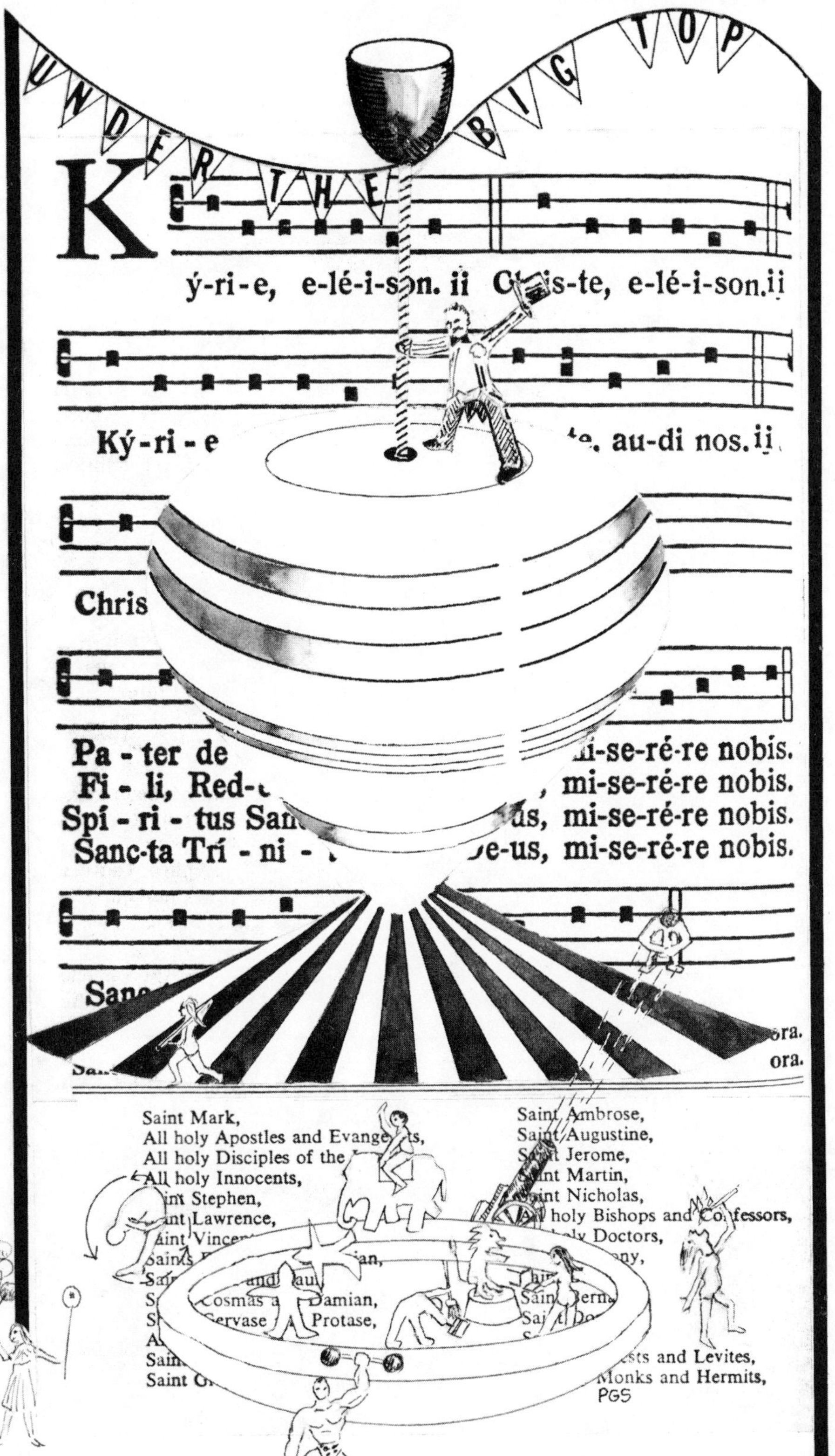
UNDER THE BIG TOP
K ý-ri-e, e-lé-i-son. ii
-s-te, e-lé-i-son. ii
Ký-ri-e
au-di nos. ii
Chris
Pa-ter de
mi-se-ré-re nobis.
Fi-li, Red-
mi-se-ré-re nobis.
Spí-ri-tus San
mi-se-ré-re nobis.
Sanc-ta Trí-ni-
mi-se-ré-re nobis.
ora.
ora.
Saint Mark,
All holy Apostles and Evange
All holy Disciples of the
All holy Innocents,
Saint Ambrose,
Saint Augustine,
Jerome,
Martin,
Nicholas,
holy Bishops and Co fessors,
holy Doctors,
Cosmas a Damian,
Gervase Protase,
Monks and Hermits,
PGS

7. The Vineyard Workers

(Matthew 20:1–15)

"The reign of God is like the case of the owner of an estate who went out at dawn to hire workmen for his vineyard. After reaching an agreement with them for the usual daily wage, he sent them out to his vineyard. He came out about midmorning and saw other men standing around the marketplace without work, so he said to them, 'You too go along to my vineyard and I will pay whatever is fair.' At that they went away. He came out again around noon and midafternoon and did the same. Finally, going out in late afternoon he found still others standing around. To these he said, 'Why have you been standing here idle all day?' 'No one has hired us,' they told him. He said, 'You go to the vineyard too.' When evening came the owner of the vineyard said to his foreman, 'Call the workmen and give them their pay, but begin with the last group and end with the first.' When those hired late in the afternoon came up they received a full day's pay, and when the first group appeared they supposed they would get more; yet they received the same daily wage. Thereupon they complained to the owner, 'This last group did only an hour's work, but you have put them on the same basis as us who have worked a full day in the scorching heat.' 'My friend,' he said to one in reply, 'I do you no injustice. You agreed on the usual wage, did you not? Take your pay and go home. I intend to give this man who was hired last the same pay as you. I am free to do as I please with my money, am I not? Or are you envious because I am generous?' "

Under the Big Top

Cast:

The Narrator	Ignatius (Human Canon Ball)
E. P. Unum	Joan the Fire Eater
Samson the Strong	Martha
Christina the Astonishing	Alphonsus
Damien the Leaper	Bosco (A Clown)
Felicitas the Fearless	Flower (A Clown)
Francis	

Narrator:

Ladies and gentlemen, children of all ages, this is the story of how a very special circus came to be. It happened, oddly enough, once upon a time in a Kingdom that was, shall we say, closer than you think.

Now in this Kingdom there lived a person named E. P. Unum. Mr. Unum had always loved the circus. He also loved children of all ages. He had a dream of putting together the greatest circus in the Kingdom. He wanted to bring together the rich variety of people and talent under ONE BIG TOP. They didn't call him Unum for nihil!

And so one day, even though it wasn't very dirty, E. P. decided to scour the Kingdom looking for different talent and acts that could be shared in his circus with all the people.

Early one morning he set out looking for acts. He came upon some people of the Kingdom and spoke to them about his dream.

Unum:

I guess you have all heard that I'm starting a circus for all the people to enjoy. Right now I need some CENTER RING acts. Are any of you experienced and interested?

Narrator:
Two people came forward. (*They are in the very front of the congregation. They keep clearing their throats. Each is vying for Unum's attention.*)

Unum:
(*To Christina and Samson*) Who are you?

Christina:
Don't you know who we are?

Unum:
I'm afraid not.

Christina:
I am Christina the Astonishing!

Samson:
I am Samson the Strong!

Christina:
I walk the high wire!

Samson:
I lift immense weights!

Unum:
Great! You'd be wonderful in my circus. Will you join?

Christina:
If I get top billing.

Samson:
If I get top billing.

Christina:
Samson:
(*They look at each other*) If *we* get top billing.

Unum:
Fine! You're both hired.

Narrator:
After some time, E. P. realized that there was room for other acts in his circus. So once again he went out in search of talent. He found three more people who wished to join his circus. (*These three come from a little further into the congregation.*)

Unum:
You, sir, who are you?

Damien:
My name is Damien.

Unum:
And what do you do?

Damien:
Why I'm Damien the Leaper! (*Unum shields his face in horror.*) No! No! That's not a disease! I'm just an acrobat.

Unum:
Oh what a relief that is! And you, madame?

Felicitas:
I'm not a madame. I'm a lion tamer. I go by "Felicitas the Fearless."

Unum:
Didn't you used to have a partner?

Felicitas:
Oh, you mean Perpetua the Pitiful. Unfortunately she was recently eaten by a new lion in the act during a two-week engagement in North Africa.

Unum:
And you, sir? You seem to have the look and smell of someone who also works very close with animals.

Francis:
(*Francis speaks with a heavy Italian accent.*) That's a right! My name, she is a Francis. There is no animal I can no tame. My specialty is a training Big Pack-a-germs!

Unum:
You mean you handle bacteria?

Francis:
No! No! Pack-a-germs! You know, Elephantes. (*Francis does an elephant noise and imitation.*)

Unum:
This is wonderful! Would you all like to join my circus?

All:
Sure!

Unum:
Then you're all hired. You can start working at once.

Narrator:
E. P. Unum was proud of all his acts. And while he was delighted in them all, he still felt there was room for more. So, he went out looking again. He discovered two very unusual acts.

Ignatius:
Don't you recognize me? We used to live together on Loyola Boulevard.

Unum:
Well, if it isn't Ignatius. You old son of a Basque! What have you been up to?

Ignatius:
I've been working on a new act. It's called THE HUMAN CANNON BALL!

Unum:
What about you, madame.

Joan:
I'm not a madame. I'm a Fire Eater. My name is Joan.

Unum:
Don't tell me. I'll bet you prefer a hot steak to a cold chop.

Joan:
Actually, I could use some Rolaids right now.

Unum:
Well, you're both hired. I think your acts will bring a real flair to the show! (*They start to walk toward the other acts. Unum notices that Ignatius is limping.*) Ignatius, what's wrong with your leg?

Ignatius:
I haven't quite perfected the act yet.

Narrator:
Sometime later, Mr. Unum decided that his circus needed some people who, while not the center of attention, could provide invaluable assistance that would allow the show to go on. So, he hired some Roustabouts.

Unum:
Folks, I need you to help me keep the show going. The jobs aren't glamorous, but they are important.

Alphonsus:
(*He and Martha come from the last part of the congregation.*) That suits me. My name is Alphonsus. But I don't know how I

could help you. My only experience has been as a Door Man at the Kingdom Inn.

Unum:
Well, I'm looking for a sanitary engineer.

Alphonsus:
I don't know if I could do that, but I'd be happy to clean up after the animals. Do you think you might have a job for my friend, Martha?

Unum:
Yes, what about you, madame, what do you do?

Martha:
Oh, a little bit of this and a little bit of that . . . probably more that than this.

Unum:
How would you like to handle the concessions for me?

Martha:
That would be great!

Narrator:
E. P. Unum felt that his circus was complete until one day when he was walking around. He was dreaming as usual. This time he was dreaming about the spectacular opening of his show. He noticed four eyes peeping into the tent.

Narrator:
(*Bosco and Flower are in the very back of the congregation.*) They were dressed in tatters and rags. (*These two are dressed as clowns.*)

Unum:
Can I help you?

Bosco:
Oh, we were just admiring your circus.

Unum:
Well, why aren't you working in the circus? There is always room for a few more.

Flower:
No one asked us to.

Unum:
What are your names?

Bosco:
My name is Bosco. This is my friend Flower. And don't make any cracks about her being "little!"

Unum:
How would you both like to work for me? (*They consider it.*) How are you with lions?

Bosco:
She's afraid of lions!

Unum:
How about the high wire?

Bosco:
Oh, she's afraid of heights!

Unum:
How about being sanitary engineers?

Flower:
He's afraid of elephant doo-doo!

Bosco:
(*He trips over himself. Flower bumps into him.*) Would you cut that out?

Unum:
Say, I've got an idea! You know, with that paint on your face,

those colorful rags and your obvious native clumsiness, you two could fill-in between the acts. You would make people laugh. How about joining my circus?

Both:
We'd love to!

Narrator:
The main acts couldn't understand why E. P. Unum was wasting his time on two low-lifers like Bosco and Flower. Their attitude was: "Who needs clowns?" They were certain that the people would be coming to see the main acts anyway.

Preparations were intensified for the grand opening of the Greatest Show in the Kingdom. Finally the opening night arrived. It was a very proud moment for E. P. Unum.

Unum:
Ladies and gentlemen, children of all ages, I am happy to present for your entertainment and delight, the Greatest Circus in the Kingdom!

(*Here a brief mime of the circus takes place. Alphonsus and Martha carry the placards. Martha brings on a placard that reads* Christina the Astonishing. *Christina mimes climbing up and then goes on the high wire. The others mime watching with their heads. The clowns cover their eyes. Christina jumps off. Circus music plays behind all of this. Alphonsus next brings a placard of* Samson the Strong. *Samson mimes the heaviness of the barbells. When he releases them, Flower goes and picks them up with no effort. Martha then brings a placard reading* Felicitas the Fearless. *The crowd reacts with fear and horror. Alphonsus brings a placard reading* Damien the Leaper. *The crowd mimes his doing a triple somersault with their heads. Martha brings a placard reading* Francis and Friends. *When Francis makes elephant noise, everyone holds their noses. Alphonsus and Martha bring on two placards reading* The High Priestess of Halitosis *and* The Human Cannon Ball. *The crowd grabs their throats in alarm as they watch Joan. Then they mime Ignatius' flight from the cannon. They wince as he goes "splat" against an object and falls to the ground.*

The clowns run over to put the fire out—with confetti in a bucket—and to pick Ignatius up and dust him off.)

Narrator:
At the end of the show, E. P. wanted to bring all of his performers out for a well-deserved round of applause. But he did it in a most unexpected way. The first people he brought out were not the main acts, but the clowns. The people greeted them warmly. (*Unum invites applause and then signals the people to stop for each act.*) Samson and Christina were amazed that they had not been called out first, as were the other acts. But what bothered them even more was that they received the same applause as everyone else. They were indignant that they had received no more than the clowns.

Unum:
Thank you, ladies and gentlemen, boys and girls. That concludes this evening's performances . . .

Samson:
(*Obviously agitated.*) Excuse me, Mr. Unum.

Unum:
Yes, Samson.

Samson:
If you don't mind my saying, sir, this is no way to end the show.

Unum:
What do you mean?

Christina:
It's not right! And it's not fair!

Unum:
I still don't know what you mean.

Samson:
We've been with the circus for some time, sir. It doesn't seem

right that we should all get the same applause. After all, we are the main acts.

Christina:
We are the ones the people came to see.

Samson:
You did make us certain promises.

Unum:
And I kept them. I promised you both top billing and I gave it to you. I just also happened to reward you all equally. And besides, if you have a complaint, I'm not the one to talk to. Have you forgotten? I'm a character in this story just like the rest of you. Talk to the person who wrote this story if you're dissatisfied.

Christina:
Well who wrote it?

Narrator:
I did! (*The Narrator steps out from the podium and moves over to the characters.*) What seems to be the problem?

Samson:
Your ending doesn't make any sense!

Narrator:
What do you mean?

Samson:
We are the main acts.

Christina:
We're more important to the circus. We did the most work.

Samson:
And besides, we've been in his circus and your story much longer than these BOZOS!

Christina:
So why do we all get the same applause? Why does it end this way?

Narrator:
E. P. Unum, what was your dream?

Unum:
To bring you all under ONE BIG TOP; to have you exercise and share and enjoy your very different talents and gifts; to have you all know there is a place for you under my tent, there is room for all of you in my circus.

Narrator:
And there's room for all of you in my story.

Unum:
You are all deserving of applause.

Christina:
It just doesn't seem fair! (*Unum looks in frustration to the Narrator for help.*)

Narrator:
You're right. It isn't fair. But who said life would be fair under the Big Top? (*The characters look embarrassed or confused or irritated respectively. Then they all freeze as the circus music comes up again.*)

Finis

Under the Big Top

Theme:
Generosity.

Props:
(1) Recorded circus music.

(2) Seven placards which read: *Christina the Astonishing, Samson the Strong, Felicitas the Fearless, Damien the Leaper, Francis and Friends, The High Priestess of Halitosis,* and *The Human Cannon Ball.*

Production Notes:
This story drama was performed on the feast of All Saints. The feast we were celebrating, as well as the particular parable we worked with, shaped this story dramatization.

Different characters wore clothing appropriate to their act. Bosco and Flower were dressed as clowns. Martha and Alphonsus were dressed in work clothes. Joan of Arc was dressed in red. Ignatius was dressed in black and wore a motorcycle helmet and black gloves.

The circus music helped create the environment of the circus. This music is especially important during the extended mime of the circus acts.

Study Questions

(1) Which character in this parable do you identify with most? Why? Explain. Which character in this parable do you identify with least? Why? Explain. What group of laborers do you identify with? Why? Reflect on what child you were in your family (i.e., the oldest, the youngest, in the middle, etc.). Do you see any relationship between this and the group of laborers with which you identified? Why or why not? Explain.

(2) What does the word generous mean? Look this word up in the dictionary. What does the word generous come from? What makes a person generous? How do you become a generous person? Do you know any generous people? What are some potential obstacles to becoming generous? Would you describe yourself as a generous person? Why or why not? Explain. What does the word pusilanimous mean? Is this the opposite of generous? Why or why not? Explain. Why is the owner in this parable

generous? Imagine yourself as the owner. Dwell in the owner's acts. What insight do you get into why the owner acts the way he or she does? Explain and share.

(3) Become one of the characters or elements in this parable for a week. Experience everything that happens from the perspective of your character or element. Record in your journal all that you think, all that you sense, all that you feel, and all that you learn as your character or element.

(4) What is justice? What is the relationship between faith and justice? Read the following pieces of Scripture: [1] Isaiah 1:16–17, [2] Micah 6:8, and [3] James 2:14–17, 26. What does it mean to make justice your aim? Is justice your aim? Why or why not? Explain. In the Isaiah reading, discuss what the "wrong," the "orphan's plea," and the "widow" symbolize for you. What wrongs need to be redressed today? How can you begin to redress them? What cries need to be heard? How can you begin to hear them? Who needs to be defended? How can you begin to defend them? Is anyone in the parable of the vineyard workers treated unjustly? Why or why not? Explain.

(5) Where is the Kingdom of God to be found? Read Luke 17:20–21. How is the Kingdom of God or Reign in your midst? What might be some signs or indications of its presence? According to an Hasidic story, a rabbi said that God dwells wherever we let God in. What part of your life do you find it most difficult to let God in? Why? Explain.

(6) Have you ever been to a circus? Did you enjoy it? What did you like about it? Why do you think E. P. Unum loved circuses? Did it have anything to do with his loving children of all ages? Why or why not? Explain. What was E. P. Unum's dream? What are some of the hopes and dreams that you have for yourself and others? Write them down in your journal. What would have to happen or what would you have to do in order for your hopes to be realized and for your dreams to come true? Why do you think E. P. Unum wanted to bring everyone together under one big top? Discuss and share.

(7) What is a saint? How many saints can you think of? Do you have a favorite saint? What do you think about them? Are you named after a saint? If so, which one? Do you know anything about the saint you are named after? Find out something about them in a book on the lives of the saints. What does your name mean? How does a name capture people's hopes and dreams for you? Explain. Who are the different people that E. P. Unum hires? Did you know that each one of them is a saint? What act does each one perform? How does what they do tell you something about who they are? Look each of these saints up in a book on the lives of the saints or in the New Catholic Encyclopedia. What do you learn about each one? What act would you be in the circus? What quality or activity most captures who you are or what saint you are called to be?

(8) Do you ever ask for or demand top-billing the way Samson and Christina do? What do you do if you don't get it? What do the other acts think of Bosco and Flower? Why do they feel this way? Listen to a recording of the song "Send In the Clowns." Why does E. P. Unum bring Bosco and Flower out first for the applause? What do you think about everyone getting the same type of applause? Do you think life is fair? Why or why not? Explain. Think of all the times you were treated better than you deserved. Write these down in your journal. Think of all the times you were treated worse than you deserved. Write these down in your journal. Samson and Christina say they deserve more applause. Do they "deserve" to be in the circus? Do you "deserve" the gift of life? Reflect on this and share.

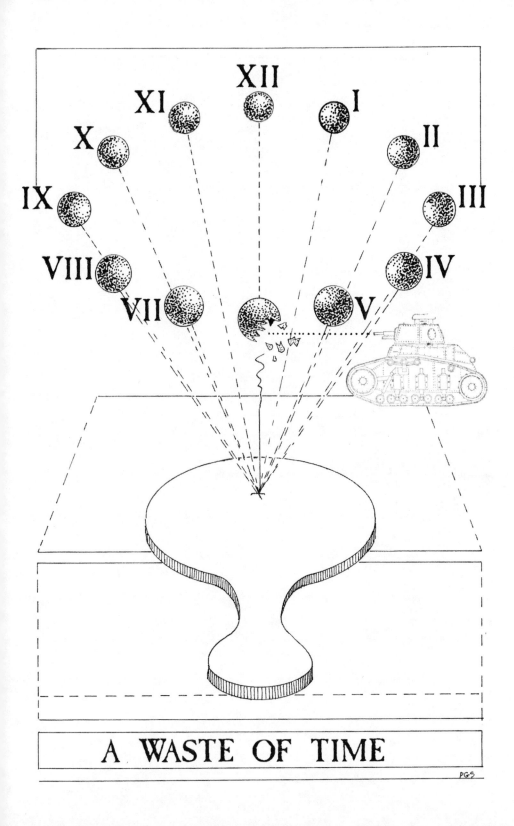

A WASTE OF TIME

8. *The Unmerciful Servant*

(Matthew 18:21–35)

Then Peter came up and asked him, "Lord, when my brother wrongs me, how often must I forgive him? Seven times?" "No," Jesus replied, "not seven times; I say, seventy times seven times. That is why the reign of God may be said to be like a king who decided to settle accounts with his officials. When he began his auditing, one was brought in who owed him a huge amount. As he had no way of paying it, his master ordered him to be sold, along with his wife, his children, and all his property, in payment of the debt. At that the official prostrated himself in homage and said, 'My lord, be patient with me and I will pay you back in full.' Moved with pity, the master let the official go and wrote off the debt. But when that same official went out he met a fellow servant who owed him a mere fraction of what he himself owed. He seized him and throttled him. 'Pay back what you owe,' he demanded. His fellow servant dropped to his knees and began to plead with him, 'Just give me time and I will pay you back in full.' But he would hear none of it. Instead, he had him put in jail until he paid back what he owed. When his fellow servants saw what had happened they were badly shaken, and went to their master to report the whole incident. His master sent for him and said, 'You worthless wretch! I canceled your entire debt when you pleaded with me. Should you not have dealt mercifully with your fellow servant, as I dealt with you?' Then in anger the master handed him over to the torturers until he paid back all that he owed. My heavenly Father will treat you exactly the same way unless each of you forgives his brother from his heart."

A Waste of Time

Cast:

Narrator

The King

The Queen

The Prince

The Princess

The Guard

The Spy

The Messenger

The Stranger

The Widow

The Orphan

Villager

Narrator:

Once upon a time—whether or not it's a waste of time is for you to decide—there lived a King and Queen. And what good would a King and Queen be without a realm? One day the Rulers of the realm called their two children together. Their children were, by some strange coincidence, the Prince and Princess.

Queen:

Children, it is time for you to assume your responsibilities for governance of the realm.

King:

What your mother means is that it is time for you two to get your acts together and take them on the road.

Queen:

We are entrusting to you the Eastern and Western Kingdoms of the realm. You will rule in our place.

King:

We're just too pooped to rule!

Queen:

You will represent us. Even though we will not be with you in person, let your people come to know us through you.

Prince:
Say no more! I know just what to do!

Princess:
Well, I don't know what to do! What do you mean?

King:
Teach your people how to be truly happy.

Prince:
And they'll be truly happy when they are productive! I'll get them up every morning at six o'clock. I'll . . .

Queen:
(*Interrupting*) They will be truly happy when you teach them how to waste time.

Princess:
But how do we teach them to do that?

King:
We can't tell you how to do it.

Queen:
Together with the members of your kingdom you must explore ways to discover for yourselves.

Prince:
I've got it! I'll get them up every morning at four o'clock. I'll . . .
(*King and Queen shake their heads.*)

King:
You must go now.

Queen:
Remember all the things we've taught you.

Princess:
Will we ever see you again?

Prince:
(*Angrily*) Shhhhhhhhhhhh! (*King and Queen look at him. The Prince becomes embarrassed.*) Shhhhhure, when will we see you again?

King:
Someday we will surprise you. We will visit both of your Kingdoms.

Queen:
Until that day, the people will come to know us through you.

Narrator:
And so the Prince and Princess left for their respective Kingdoms. The Princess for the Eastern Kingdom and the Prince for the Western Kingdom. Both went about governing their people. Both had different struggles trying to honor their parents' wishes.

The Princess had a very hard time discovering how to teach the people of her Kingdom "to waste time."

Princess:
(*Pacing nervously*) Hummm! Hummm! There's got to be a way!

Villager:
What's the matter, Princess?

Princess:
I'm trying to think of some important ways to waste time.

Villager:
Why don't you take your mind off of that for a while by playing with this. (*The Villager gives her a paddle-ball.*)

Princess:
No. Thanks anyway.

Villager:
Do you want to sit down and talk about it?

Princess:
No, both of those would just be wastes of . . . (*It dawns on her.*)
You know something? That's exactly what we need to do.

Narrator:
And that was just the beginning of how the Princess and the
people of the Eastern Kingdom discovered ways of wasting time.
They gradually learned how to rest, to relax, how to play, how to
laugh and cry, how to tell stories, how to dream and hope, how
to savor and share experiences and feelings and friendship.

The Prince, who ruled the Western Kingdom, took a very
different approach.

Prince:
Rise and shine everybody! Rise and shine! All right, you sleepy
sots, wake up!

Guard:
But what time is it?

Prince:
It's time to get up and get out of bed! It's four o'clock! How
much more time are you going to waste? Are you going to sleep
your lives away?

Narrator:
The Prince thought that his parents' wish to teach the people of
his Kingdom how to waste time was utter foolishness. The Prince
was certain that the key to happiness, his own and those he ruled,
was productivity.

And so, the Prince forced his people to be productive. Now
some very strange things happened as a result of this. The more
the people produced, the more protective they became of what
they had. The people of the Prince's Kingdom committed a lot of
time and resources in order to defend themselves and all they
had. And the more they had, the more they feared those who had
little or nothing.

Stranger:
(*To Prince who is surprised by him*) Hello, there.

Prince:
Ohhhhhhhhhhh, you must be new to the Kingdom.

Stranger:
That's right. And who are you?

Prince:
The people around here simply call me "Prince."

Stranger:
Happy to meet you, Mr. Prince.

Prince:
I'm sure. And I suppose I could call you "stranger."

Stranger:
That's right! That's what I am, a stranger.

Prince:
Well strangers are a constant source of danger in my Kingdom! I sentence you to life in prison. Guard, take him away! (*The Guard takes him away. The Prince notices an orphan standing idle.*) And what do we have here?

Orphan:
An orphan, sire.

Prince:
Why aren't you working?

Orphan:
I'm too young to work.

Prince:
You're never too young.

Orphan:
Well, nobody has hired me.

Prince:
You don't work because you don't want to work. You have a very poor attitude for my Kingdom. Therefore, I sentence you to life in prison. Guard, take him away! (*The Guard starts to take the Orphan away. The Widow comes to the defense of the Orphan.*)

Widow:
Wait a minute! You can't do that to this young child!

Prince:
Who says I can't? Who are you?

Guard:
She's the widow, sire.

Prince:
Well, widow, you are wasting your breath and my time. You are also contributing to the delinquency of a minor. That is criminal. I shall have to think of a very special punishment for you. I've got it! I sentence you to life in prison! Guard, take them away! (*The Guard takes them away.*)

Narrator:
The more the Prince built up the defenses of his Kingdom, the more fearful he became of what was going on in his sister's Kingdom. So he sent a spy to see what was going on. She took very detailed notes about everything she observed. She saw someone playing with a paddle-ball and was intrigued.

Spy:
What's that you have there?

Villager:
I've never seen you here before. Welcome, stranger!

Spy:
Never mind that nonsense! What do you have there—a new kind of weapon?

Villager:
No, it's not a weapon. It's a toy.

Spy:
What do you do with it?

Villager:
We play with it here in our Kingdom. Don't you know how to play?

Spy:
My work is my play! That is a waste of time.

Villager:
That's right! Why, you're pulling my leg, aren't you? You have played before.

Spy:
Never! (*Still intrigued by it*) However, I would appreciate one of these for observation. (*The Villager gives the Spy a paddle-ball. The Villager leaves. The Spy gradually begins playing with it and enjoying it.*)

Narrator:
When the Prince's spy returned, she reported all that she had seen and heard.

Spy:
Sire, I swear that these people don't have any defenses. They spend their time in many different ways enjoying themselves.

Prince:
(*The Prince grabs the paddle-ball. He hits himself trying to use it.*) You don't call this a weapon? Your shoddy report has wasted my

time. Therefore, you guessed it, I sentence you to life in prison! Guard, take her away! (*The Guard takes her away. The Prince throws the paddle-ball away in disgust.*)

Narrator:
Meanwhile, in the Eastern Kingdom, the Princess had discovered a wonderful new way of wasting time. It was called "having a banquet." She wished to share her discovery with her brother and the people of the Western Kingdom. So she sent a trusted messenger to invite them to join her for a feast.

Prince:
(*Messenger walks in using a paddle-ball.*) What do you think you're doing? Where did you get that?

Messenger:
Wait a minute. I'm almost up to fifty.

Prince:
What's the meaning of this? Who are you?

Messenger:
I'm a messenger from your sister. She has sent me to invite you and all the people of your Kingdom to a banquet.

Prince:
If my sister thinks that I would fall into a trap like that, she's wasting her time. Would you quit hitting that ball?

Messenger:
Well, what should I tell her?

Prince:
You'll tell her nothing! For wasting my time, I sentence you to— I've got just the punishment for you—life in prison! Guard, take him away. (*The Guard comes to take the Messenger.*)

Narrator:
As they moved toward the prison, the messenger gave his paddle-

ball to the Guard. The Guard was delighted and immediately began playing with it. He was so fascinated with this new toy that he completely forgot about the Messenger. The Messenger quickly made his way out of the Western Kingdom. He decided that this was so important that he should inform the King and Queen themselves about the state of affairs in the Western Kingdom.

The King and Queen could hardly believe their ears. They decided it was time for them to visit both Kingdoms. They also decided to go in disguise. (*Here the King and Queen put on clown noses and outfits and carry a paddle-ball.*)

When they arrived in the Eastern Kingdom, they were warmly welcomed. People stopped what they were doing to talk or play or laugh with them. The Princess and her people were surprised and delighted when they discovered that these strangers were really the King and Queen. The Princess shared with them the new way they had discovered of wasting time by holding a banquet in their honor. Her parents were very happy.

The Messenger told the Princess all that had happened. The King and Queen shared their concern about the Prince and his people. So, the next day, the King, the Queen and the Messenger left for the Western Kingdom. When they reached it, they found the streets empty.

King:
Where is everyone?

Queen:
The Kingdom looks deserted.

Messenger:
I'll bet the Prince is behind this.

Prince:
You called? (*Recognizing the Messenger*) You won't get away so easily this time. Do you have a license to carry a weapon?

Messenger:
I don't carry a weapon.

Prince:
Ha Ha! Then what do you call this? (*The Prince grabs a paddle-ball out of the Messenger's belt.*) And who are these fools?

King:
(*Indicating "quiet" to the Messenger*) We're strangers here.

Prince:
Dressed for a costume ball, eh? Well, those are a waste of time. And strangers are a constant source of danger here. All of you, come with me. (*They follow the Prince to the prison. There all of the people of the Kingdom are locked up. The Guard is inside playing with a paddle-ball. The Prince angrily addresses him.*) I warned you to stop that! Well, I've got some new playmates for you. I sentence the three of you to life in prison!

King:
What for?

Prince:
For wasting time!

Queen:
And all of these other people, why are they here?

Prince:
In one way or another, for wasting time!

Queen:
(*Looking at the King*) This must stop at once! (*The Queen and King pull off their clown noses.*)

Prince:
(*Gasping*) Mother! Father! I think I'm going to be sick. Listen, I know this looks bad, but I can explain everything!

King:
Enough! Silence! People of the Kingdom, our son, the Prince, has been very wicked. We entrusted you to him and instructed him to

teach you all how to waste time. He has done us a great disservice and you a great wrong.

Queen:
Messenger, release the prisoners! (*The Messenger takes the keys from the Prince. After the Messenger lets all the prisoners out he gives the keys to the Guard.*) People of the Western Kingdom, we invite you to join us and begin again.

King:
Come with us and learn to live another way.

Queen:
Our daughter has prepared a banquet for all of you. Come. Eat. Drink. Learn what the Prince would not, could not teach you.

Narrator:
The King and Queen began moving toward the huge door of the Western Kingdom. The people looked at the prince and then at one another. Slowly they began to follow the King and Queen, one by one. Only the Prince remained. (*The Guard is the last one to leave. He gives the keys of the Prison to the Prince. Then the Guard gives the Prince his paddle-ball.*)

King:
Will you come with us, son?

Prince:
Don't be ridiculous! It would be a waste of time!

Queen:
Won't you change your mind and join us?

Prince:
Not on your life! Go on, all of you, get out of here! (*The King and Queen and all the people turn and leave. The Prince mimes barring the door.*)

Narrator:
The King and Queen were very sad. Heavy-hearted, they led the people into the Kingdom of the Princess and the new way of life that awaited them. They knew they could only hope, now, and wait for the Prince. (*The Prince has been looking at the paddle-ball. He tries it again and hits himself. He throws down the paddle-ball in disgust.*)

Finis

A Waste of Time

Theme:
Forgiveness.

Props:
(1) Two crowns—one for the King and one for the Queen.
(2) Eleven paddles and balls.
(3) One set of prison keys.
(4) Two clown noses—one for the King and one for the Queen.
(5) Two simple clown disguises—one for the King and one for the Queen.
(6) One prison door facade made out of wood or heavy cardboard.

Production Notes:
The Eastern and the Western Kingdoms can each occupy half of your stage area. When action takes place in the Eastern Kingdom, the inhabitants of the Western Kingdom "freeze." This means they are still. When action shifts to the Western Kingdom, the inhabitants of the Eastern Kingdom "freeze."

Study Questions

(1) St. Ignatius of Loyola, in his classic work *The Spiritual Exercises,* suggests a method of scriptural prayer that involves

our imaginations. He invites us to place ourselves in a biblical scene; to see the persons in the scene; to consider, observe and contemplate what they are saying and doing; then, to reflect and draw some fruit from what we have observed and overheard. Try this method of prayer with this biblical story. Become one of the fellow servants who is an observer to all of the action. What does the Master evoke in you? What does the first servant evoke in you? What does the second servant evoke in you? Is your life changed as a result of what you experience? Why or why not? If it is changed, how is it changed?

(2) Reflect on your personal experiences of forgiving others and being forgiven by others. What thoughts, feelings and body sensations do you associate with each of these experiences? What does forgiveness mean to you? How do you forgive? How would you describe your relationship to the person who forgives you? How would you describe your relationship to the person whom you forgive? Do you believe that "Love means never having to say you're sorry"? Why or why not? What do the words "mercy" and "justice" mean to you? What do you discover about "mercy," "justice," and "forgiveness" in this passage from Scripture and from this story drama? Discuss.

(3) In verse 27 the word "compassion" appears. The Ruler has compassion. The Greek word is "splagchnizomai" which means to have the bowels yearn, that is, to feel sympathy, to pity. What does the Master leave out of his recounting of this experience in verse 33? Can you forgive without compassion? Is the first servant's failure that he/she didn't forgive another's debt or that he/she didn't have compassion? Could the inability to forgive be a symptom of something more fundamental that is missing in a person? Use your imagination and consider why the Master had compassion for the first servant. Spend some time trying to get in touch with and understand the Master's anger. Discuss.

(4) This is a Kingdom parable. What in this parable gives you a clue about the Kingdom of God and how that Kingdom comes into our lives and our hearts? Reflect on this parable in the light of Matthew 5:7: "Blessed are the merciful for they shall obtain mercy." Discuss.

(5) Examine the similarities between the scene in this story with the Ruler and the first servant, and the scene in this story with the first servant and the fellow servant. What similarities or parallels do you notice between the first and second servant's situations? What is the precise wording of each servant's request for patience and time? Mircea Eliade has pointed out that the real sin for primitive people was to forget. While this principally referred to their "myths" and "stories" it could be extended, in this situation, to "the forgiveness I have experienced." Would you expect the very wording of the second servant's request to touch off memory in the first servant of what had recently happened to him/her? Why doesn't the first servant grant the second servant's request? Reflect and discuss. Is the first servant's real sin forgetfulness? Can one be genuinely grateful if one is not mindful? Can you give thanks if you don't remember? Consider the ways that Christians "remember" and "give thanks." Discuss.

(6) What do the King and Queen want their children to teach the people of their Kingdoms? What does it mean "to waste time"? What do you think the King and Queen understand by this phrase? What does the Prince understand by this phrase? What does the Princess understand by this phrase? What ways do the people discover and explore for "wasting time"? Can you think of any other important ways of "wasting time"? What words would you use to describe the Eastern Kingdom? What words would you use to describe the Western Kingdom? Can one be "productive" and still develop the capacity to "waste time"? How do you accomplish a balance? Discuss.

(7) The King and Queen tell their children to represent them in the Eastern and Western Kingdoms of the realm. They want the people of these Kingdoms to come to know them through their children. What image or experience would the inhabitants of the Eastern Kingdom have of the King and Queen because of the Princess? Explain. What image or experience would the inhabitants of the Western Kingdom have of the King and Queen because of the Prince? Explain. What are some of the images or experiences you have of God because of Jesus? Explain. What

qualities of God did Jesus reveal? Discuss. What image, experience or impression do those around you have of Jesus and Christianity because of what you reveal through your actions and words? Explain and discuss.

(8) Is forgiveness a "waste of time"? Why or why not? Do you need to forgive yourself for any way you have wronged yourself? If you do, in your imagination do this with compassion and gentleness. Is there anyone currently in your life whom you need to forgive? Whom? Why? If you can't forgive him/her, why can't you? If you can forgive him/her, imagine yourself forgiving him/her from your heart. Is there anyone from your past whom you need to forgive? See if you can go back in your memory and forgive him/her. Don't rush this process. Unforgiven memories are memories in need of healing. In your journal, list those things that are most important to you and that give your life meaning. Then figure out how your average day and week are spent. How much time do you give each day and week to those things you listed as most important in giving your life meaning? If you are not spending much time with them, how could you spend more time with them? Discuss.

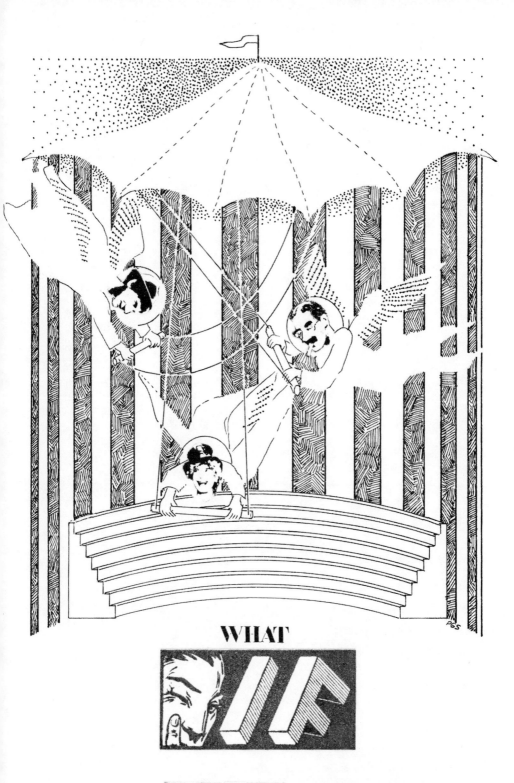

WHAT **IF** YOU GAVE A CIRCUS & NOBODY CAME?

9. The Wedding Banquet

(Matthew 22:1–14)

Jesus began to address them, once more using parables. "The reign of God may be likened to the king who gave a wedding banquet for his son. He dispatched his servants to summon the invited guests to the wedding but they refused to come. A second time he sent other servants, saying: 'Tell those who are invited, See, I have my dinner prepared! My bullocks and corn-fed cattle are killed; everything is ready. Come to the feast.' Some ignored the invitation and went their way, one to his farm, another to his business. The rest laid hold of his servants, insulted them, and killed them. At this the king grew furious and sent his army to destroy those murderers and burn their city. Then he said to his servants: 'The banquet is ready, but those who were invited were unfit to come. That is why you must go out into the byroads and invite to the wedding anyone you come upon.' The servants then went out into the byroads and rounded up everyone they met, bad as well as good. This filled the wedding hall with banqueters.

"When the king came to meet the guests, however, he caught sight of a man not properly dressed for a wedding feast. 'My friend,' he said, 'how is it you came in here not properly dressed?' The man had nothing to say. The king then said to the attendants, 'Bind him hand and foot and throw him out into the night to wail and grind his teeth.' "

What If You Gave a Circus
and Nobody Came?

Cast:

Narrator	Air-1 (woman)
King Frederick	Air-2 (man)
Queen Ethel	Air-3 (woman)
Princess Minnie	Air-4 (man)
Messenger-1	Earth-1 (woman)
Messenger-2	Earth-2 (man)
Messenger-3	Earth-3 (woman)
	Earth-4 (man)

[*The Messengers are modeled after the three Marx Brothers. Messenger-1 is modeled after Groucho. Messenger-2 is modeled after Chico. Messenger-3 is modeled after Harpo. If possible, try to have your Messengers dress like the Marx Brothers.*]

Narrator:
Once upon a time, there was a Kingdom called Mirth. (*The three Messengers blow party horns and throw confetti.*) The Kingdom was inhabited by the high-born and the low-born. All were ruled by good King Frederick and Queen Ethel the Unleaded. The King and Queen had a daughter named Princess Minnie.

When the inhabitants of the Kingdom saw the Princess (*Messenger-3 takes out a saw and goes after the baby; Messenger-1 and Messenger-2 restrain him*), they all rejoiced. (*All the inhabitants blow party horns and throw confetti.*) The people brought the little Princess gifts of goldfish, frankfurters and mirth. She kept the mirth.

The King and Queen decided that on Princess Minnie's twenty-first birthday, she would begin her reign. (*The three messengers all take out their umbrellas.*) No. No. I mean, she'd become a ruler. (*Messenger-3 takes out a tape measure and sizes the Princess up.*)

To commemorate this great event, the King and Queen arranged for a Coronation Circus. When the great day arrived, they sent three Royal Messengers (*Messenger-1 wears a shirt with "UNI" written on it; Messenger-2 wears a shirt with "ROY" written on it; Messenger-3 wears a shirt with "AL" written on it*) to invite all the high-born of the Kingdom who were known as Friends of the Air. (*These four Air people climb up their ladders.*)

Messenger-1:
(*To Air-1*) Is there a full moon tonight or did you just scrub your face?

Air-1:
I beg your pardon?

Messenger-1:
Go on, beg, plead, gnash your teeth if you like. Perhaps you could grovel! But what really gets me is when you say "Pretty please with strawberries on top."

Air-1:
What do you want?

Messenger-1:
What do you have?

Air-1:
Well, I've never!

Messenger-1:
Neither have I, but I'm willing to try!

Air-1:
I beg your pardon?

Messenger-1:
Oh no! Let's not start that again!

Air-1:
Who sent you?

Messenger-1:
The King and Queen!

Air-1:
What do they want?

Messenger-1:
What do you have?

Air-1:
I beg your pardon?

Messenger-1:
Do you believe in *déjà vu?*

Air-1:
Yes!

Messenger-1:
Do you believe in circuses?

Air-1:
I certainly do not?

Messenger-1:
But the King and Queen have invited you to the Coronation
Circus they are throwing for their daughter.

Air-1:
I don't believe in circuses!

Messenger-1:
Well, maybe they don't believe in you. Have you ever asked
them?

Air-1:
I'm not going. So, please go away and leave me alone! (*Messenger-1 and Air-1 freeze.*)

Messenger-2:
Hey, you up there! Do you know how to play the game "Knock, Knock"?

Air-2:
Why yes, I do.

Messenger-2:
O.K., then you start.

Air-2:
Knock. Knock.

Messenger-2:
Who's there?

Air-2:
(*Silence. Air-2 is confused.*)

Messenger-2:
Well?

Air-2:
How should I know who's there?

Messenger-2:
Why did you knock, then?

Air-2:
Because you told me to.

Messenger-2:
Well, next time don't start something you can't finish! Here. (*Messenger-2 gives Air-2 a carnation flower.*)

Air-2:
What's this for?

Messenger-2:
The King and Queen invite you to the Coronation. There'll be a Circus and everything.

Air-2:
As much as I respect the King and Queen, I'm tired of their childishness. I have more important things to do with my life. So please, go away!

Messenger-2:
Which way?

Air-2:
Any way! Just get out of here! (*Messenger-2 and Air-2 freeze.*)

Messenger-3:
(*Messenger-3 honks his horn. Air-3 looks down her ladder. Messenger-3 gestures to her to come down. Air-3 goes down to last step of her ladder. Messenger-3 sticks out his hand. Air-3 sticks out her hand. Messenger-3 puts his bent leg into her hand. Air-3 pushes it away, annoyed.*)

Air-3:
What do you want?

Messenger-3:
(*Messenger-3 unrolls a scroll and begins mouthing words. No noise comes out of his mouth.*)

Air-3:
What are you trying to say?

Messenger-3:
(*Messenger-3 hands Air-3 the scroll.*)

Air-3:
(*Air-3 begins reading the scroll.*) This is too long! (*Messenger-3 takes out a pair of scissors and cuts the scroll in half. Air-3 finishes it. She wraps it up and hands it to Messenger-3. Her hand is on the bottom of the scroll. There ensues a game of hand on top of hand. Messenger-3 loses. Air-3 throws the scroll at Messenger-3 in disgust. Messenger-3 puts up his fists to fight.*) I don't have time to attend a Circus! (*Messenger-3 gives her a watch.*) No. No. You don't understand. I mean I have more important issues to attend to. (*Messenger-3 takes out a Kleenex box and starts pulling out tissues and letting them fall to the ground.*) I'm writing a position paper for the Friends of the Air on the need for universal kindness. Now get lost! (*Messenger-3 looks confused. He joins Messenger-1 and Messenger-2 at the ladder of Air-4. They briefly jostle over who is going to invite Air-4.*)

Messenger-1:
Wait a minute! Wait a minute! Let's flip a coin. Heads I win. Tails you lose. (*Messenger-1 flips the coin.*) Heads! I win. Ahemmmmmmmm!

Air-4:
How do you do.

Messenger-1:
That's a fine "How do you do!" How I do and what I do is none of your business! But let's not split hairs. (*Messenger-3 pulls out a rabbit and a hatchet.*)

Messengers:
On behalf of the King and Queen, we invite you to come to the Circus.

Air-4:
No thank you.

Messenger-1:
No, thank *you.*

Air-4:
NO THANK YOU!

Messenger-2:
No. No. No. THANK *YOU!*

Air-4:
Look, I'm busy. Don't bother me. Why don't you invite the Friends of the Earth. They have nothing better to do!

Narrator:
And so, the Royal Messengers returned to the King and Queen empty-handed. (*The Messengers all show their empty hands. Messenger-3 pulls out his pockets and shows his empty pockets.*)

Queen:
They all refused? (*The Messengers all shake their heads "Yes."*)

King:
That's a fine "How do you do!"

Messenger-1:
How do you do!

Narrator:
The King and the Queen were so disappointed in the refusals of the high-born that they resolved never to be called "Their Highnesses" again. (*The King and Queen leave their thrones and go sit on a step.*) They decreed that henceforth they would be referred to as "Their Lownesses." Once again they sent out their Royal Messengers. Only this time they sent them to bring in the Friends of the Earth. (*Here a brief mime begins. Messenger-1 gets Earth-1 to come to the Circus by leading her there with a carrot on a stick. Messenger-2 forces Earth-2 to the Circus at blunderbuss [rifle]-point. Messenger-3 brings Earth-3 to the Circus in a huge butterfly net. Then the three Messengers see Earth-4. They carry him to the Circus over their heads.*)

Messenger-1:
On behalf of their Royal Lownesses, Fred and Ethel, I welcome you with open arms to this Coronation Circus.

Messenger-2:
How late do you stay open?

Earth-1:
We're grateful for the invitation . . .

Earth-2:
But we're not dressed for a Circus.

Earth-3:
We're not dressed for anything! (*Messenger-3 pulls out a huge dress, then a paper sack. Finally, he shows them some clown noses. Messenger-2 gives one to Earth-1, Earth-2, and Earth-3. They all put them on. Messenger-2 offers a clown nose to Earth-4.*)

Earth-4:
No thank you!

Messenger-1:
No, thank *you!*

Earth-4:
NO THANK YOU!

Messenger-2:
No. No. No. THANK YOU!

Earth-4:
You don't understand. I'm not about to put that silly nose on!

Narrator:
Everything was prepared now. The Circus was ready to begin. The Messengers ushered in the King and Queen. (*Messenger-3 pinches the Queen who yells "Owwwww!" The King and Queen have red noses on.*) Fred and Ethel welcomed each of their guests

warmly. When they discovered one of the guests without a nose, they were shocked.

King:
Friend, where is your nose? (*Earth-4 looks embarrassed.*)

Queen:
Perhaps he was overlooked. Here, I have another. (*The Queen puts a red nose on Earth-4. He looks at the King and Queen, pulls off the nose, throws it down on the ground and leaves. He goes to a ladder and climbs it.*)

King:
Bring in Princess Minnie. (*The Messengers bring her in. She is dressed in a clown outfit. Messenger-3 pinches her. She yells "Owwwwwww!" Since everyone is ready, let the Circus begin.*)

Messenger-3:
(*Messenger-3 finally notices the congregation. He whistles and honks his horn to get the King's and Queen's attention.*)

King:
What's the matter? (*Messenger-3 points to the congregation.*)

Princess:
Mother. Father. Look at all of them. Why can't these people join us? There's plenty of room for them under our Circus tent.

Queen:
They can . . .

King:
Provided . . . (*The King calls the three Messengers to him. He whispers in their ears. They nod their assent. Then all three Messengers go and extend a red nose in the general area of the congregation. They all freeze.*)

Finis

What If You Gave a Circus and Nobody Came?

Theme:
Invitation to Relationship.

Props:
(1) Seven Party Horns.
(2) One bag of confetti.
(3) One small hand saw.
(4) Two goldfish which are cut out of cardboard and wrapped in gold foil. They hang from a piece of string.
(5) Three frankfurters linked together.
(6) One laughing box.
(7) Three umbrellas.
(8) Three shirts with "Uni" written on the first, "ROY" written on the second, and "AL" written on the third.
(9) Four ladders of different heights.
(10) One carnation flower.
(11) One bicycle horn a la Harpo Marx.
(12) One scroll.
(13) One pair of scissors.
(14) One large plastic pocket watch.
(15) One box of tissues.
(16) One large coin made from the plastic cover of a coffee can and covered with tinfoil.
(17) One stuffed rabbit.
(18) One hatchet.
(19) One carrot hanging from a stick.
(20) One plastic blunderbuss.
(21) One huge butterfly net.
(22) Eight red clown noses.
(23) Two crowns.

Production Notes:
The three messengers are supposed to resemble the three Marx Brothers. Princess Minnie is dressed like a clown. The King and Queen are dressed nicely and wear a crown.

Since the original parable is about a banquet, the celebration of the Eucharist would be particularly appropriate after this story drama proclamation.

Study Questions

(1) Have you ever been invited to a party? What are the best parties that you have been to? What was it about these parties that made them so good? Write down the special characteristics in your journal. What are some of the worst parties you have attended? Why were they so bad? What was missing? Write these qualities down in your journal. Can the properties of a really good party or meal give you any clues about the Kingdom of God? Why or why not? Explain. Has anyone ever given you an invitation which you refused? Why did you refuse? Has anyone ever turned down an invitation which you made to him or her? How did you feel? What do the excuses in this parable symbolize? What are some of the ways you are unable to respond to the invitation of God's Word? In what ways are the Word of God and the invitation in the Kingdom of God inconvenient in your life? Explain.

(2) Experience this story for the perspective of the different characters. Be the King in your imagination. Why do you throw this party? Whom do you invite? What are you thinking, feeling and sensing when you invite the original people? Dwell in the King's acts. What insight do you get into who the King is and why he does what he does? Be one of the people who refuse the King's invitation. What are your excuses? Why don't you accept? Dwell in this person's acts. What insight do you get into him or her? Be one of the people from the byroads who is rounded up to become a banqueter. Did you expect to be invited? Dwell in this person's acts. What insight do you get into what this person thinks, feels, and senses? Finally, be the banqueter who doesn't have a wedding garment. Dwell in this person's acts. Why aren't

you wearing a wedding garment? What insight do you get into what this person thinks, feels and senses?

(3) What does the wedding banquet symbolize for you? Do you think that the King acted harshly toward the person who wasn't wearing a wedding garment? Why or why not? Explain. In ancient times, people would be given a wedding garment as part of the invitation to the banquet. The person without the garment somehow refused the garment offered. What was this person refusing? Can you think of any sacrament where putting on a new garment is part of the ritual? What about baptism? What does the garment symbolize in this sacrament? What are the ways that you resist personal transformation in your life?

(4) What does the word conversion mean? Look this word up in your dictionary. What does the word conversion come from? What are we supposed to turn toward or to as Christians? Turning toward someone or something implies turning away from something else. What are we supposed to turn away from? How do you accomplish both the "turning away from" and the "turning toward" in your life? Read Mark 1:14–15. Jesus' proclamation is twofold: [1] repent, and [2] believe in the good news. What does it mean to repent? How have you expressed repentance in your life? Where in your life do you need repentance now? What is the good news? What does it mean to believe in the good news? How have you experienced the good news in your life? What parts of your life are most in need of the good news? Explain.

(5) How do you experience the presence of God in your life? How might God be present in waitings, longings, and interruptions? What does God invite you to? Have you ever thought or felt that God's invitations to you come at the wrong time or in the wrong place? Why or why not? Explain. How does God sneak into your life in unexpected ways? Do you become vulnerable when you invite? Do you become vulnerable when you accept? What does the banquet in this parable symbolize for you? In what way can every invitation be an invitation to relationship? Reflect on the different relationships in your life. Reread this

parable. Experience the King's invitations to the banquet as invitations to relationship. Why would you accept? Why would you refuse? What obstacles and fears would you personally have to deal with in order to accept an invitation to relationship? Once you've accepted, how does the relationship deepen and grow?

(6) Who were the Friends of the Air? Who were the Friends of the Earth? How do the Friends of the Air respond to the King's and Queen's invitations? Why do they refuse? How do the Friends of the Earth respond to the invitations? What are their fears? Who or what do the Friends of the Air and the Friends of the Earth symbolize for you? Which group do you identify with? Explain.

(7) What does the word mirth mean? Look this word up in the dictionary. Do you have a good sense of humor? Why or why not? Explain. In the play *A Thousand Clowns,* Murray says that his nephew has a good eye for street humor. Do you have a good eye for humor? Can you see humor in other people's lives? Can you see humor in your own life? Where do you see humor in your own life? What does the word angel mean? Look this word up in the dictionary. What did you think of the Messengers in this story drama? In your journal list all the different ways that God figuratively speaks to you. Do you think that you ever ignore or dismiss the Word of God because of the way that it comes to you? Why or why not? Explain. Read Isaiah 55:6–11 in light of both this parable and this story drama. Reflect and share.

(8) What do the red noses symbolize for you? Why does the one Friend of the Earth refuse to put on a clown nose? At the end of the story drama, The Messengers offer a red nose to all those listening and watching. Would you accept a clown nose? Why or why not? Explain. St. Paul, in 1 Corinthians 4:10, says that we are "fools for Christ's sake." What do you think St. Paul means by this? How are we supposed to be fools for Christ? Read 2 Corinthians 6:1–13. In what ways might St. Paul's description here be the biography of a clown? Explain. Read Mary's *Magnificat* in Luke 1:46–55. In what ways is this the prayer of clowns? Explain.

10. The Lost Sheep

(Matthew 18:10–14)

"See that you never despise one of these little ones. I assure you, their angels in heaven constantly behold my heavenly Father's face. What is your thought on this: a man owns a hundred sheep and one of them wanders away; will he not leave the ninety-nine out on the hills and go in search of the stray? If he succeeds in finding it, believe me, he is happier about this one than about the ninety-nine that did not wander away. Just so, it is no part of your heavenly Father's plan that a single one of these little ones shall ever come to grief."

Lost and Found

Narrator:
In the beginning, when the Kingdom was very young, the earth was filled with forests and meadows. It was at this time that Mother Nature began gathering together animals of all kinds. She was careful to see that no animal was excluded. She delighted in the amazing variety of her creatures. Each was beautiful and gifted in its own way.

There was the Eagle who was strong and determined. He was a natural leader, if a bit defensive at times.

Eagle:
Hey, what do you mean by that?

Narrator:
Then there was the Bee who was very efficient.

Bee:
Efficient. E-F-F-I-C-I-E-N-T. Efficient!

Narrator:
This was no ordinary Bee. This was a spelling Bee. There was also a Squirrel who was very industrious—and a little nuts.

Squirrel:
Peanuts. Walnuts. Cashews. Macadamia Nuts. Coconuts. Did someone say Coconuts? (*Groucho Marx style.*)

Narrator:
Mother Nature had an eye for beauty, so she included the stately Peacock in her family of animals. She also included the speedy, if a bit independent, Ostrich. (*The Ostrich comes in wearing a jogging suit and carrying a pail or bucket.*) Mother Nature knew how serious and preoccupied animals can be at times and so she invited the Monkey to join her little family. She also invited the Turtle. (*Nothing happens.*) She also invited the Turtle!

Turtle:
I'm coming! I'm coming! You want I should get an ulcer?

Narrator:
You see, the Turtle was a little slow. Then there was the Spider who wasn't particularly good at knitting but who could spin a yarn so interesting that it would bring all who heard it together. There was also the Owl.

All:
Who?

Narrator:
The Owl. Now the Owl, whose vision had dimmed, depended more on insight than eyesight. And last, but not least, Mother Nature invited a creature of a different stripe. (*All start smelling themselves.*) One who created quite a stink. (*Mother Nature puts a clothes pin on her nose and beckons Skunk up. Skunk is spraying herself with an atomizer.*) She was the Skunk.

Mother Nature loved all the creatures, no matter what their limitations. Each one was unique and special to her.

Mother:
I've brought you all together from different parts of the Kingdom for a very special reason.

Eagle:
For what purpose? I was doing fine by myself.

Mother:
I want you to live together and learn how to become a family.

Skunk:
Great! Ooh! Ooh! How about a family picture?

Peacock:
That idea stinks!

Turtle:
Stinks? I think it's wonderful! I'll be in the front!

Bee:
Do we have enough time for this?

Owl:
What?

Bee:
Time. T-I-M-E Time!

Ostrich:
I knew this was a bad idea! (*Ostrich puts pail over his head.*)

Monkey:
(*To Ostrich*) Are you nuts?

Squirrel:
Nuts? Nuts? Get your peanuts, walnuts, coconuts, here!

Monkey:
(*To Squirrel*) You're nuts! He's bananas!

Spider:
You know, this reminds me of a great story. Once upon a time
. . .

Bee:
I don't have time for this.

Mother:
(*She waves her wand but nothing happens. Then she blows a whistle and gets their attention.*) Learning to live together will take time. In your case, lots of time. It is, however, important. I can think of no better way to start your life together than with a family picture. So, gather together now. (*They do so reluctantly.*) Everybody smile. (The Monkey gets out of the picture and pinches Mother Nature while she's arranging people.) Ooooooooohhh! (*She sees Monkey. There is a thunder sound effect.*) It's not nice to fool Mother Nature. (*Monkey gets back in the picture.*) Smile.

Narrator:
Mother Nature left. And soon the picture changed. (*Everyone starts choking one another.*) The Eagle, the Bee, the Peacock, the Squirrel and the Ostrich soon discovered they had little in common with the others. While they were industrious and efficient . . .

All:
Efficient. E-F-F-I-C-I-E-N-T. Efficient!

Narrator:
They found the others a troublesome and useless burden. (*Ostrich puts pail over his head.*)

Spider:
It will be difficult to become a family if we are constantly at one another's throats. Let's remember what Mother Nature gathered us together for.

Eagle:
Let's remember that your long-winded stories are a waste of time!

Turtle:
Wait a minute! Wait a minute! What family doesn't have its ups

and downs? There's got to be give and take. (*Turtle reaches for some of the Squirrel's nuts.*)

Squirrel:
Yeah! We give and you take!

Monkey:
(*Goes to Squirrel.*) Aren't we taking this all a bit too seriously? (*Monkey tries to steal some nuts. Monkey gives nuts to Turtle. Bee comes over and takes the nuts back to Squirrel and slaps Monkey's paw.*)

Bee:
Stop. S-T-O-P. Stop all this Monkey business!

Peacock:
All you tactless and rude animals can do is ruffle our feathers! And who needs that?

Owl:
I think you're looking at this with the wrong eyes.

Peacock:
How would you know? You're blind as a bat!

Skunk:
What's the big stink about? (*Holding up picture.*) Remember, we're a family!

Ostrich:
Who needs that?

All:
We do! We do! (*Said by Spider and companions.*)

All:
Well, I don't! (*Said by Eagle and companions.*)

Narrator:
And so the Eagle and his companions left. But the only place
they could go to escape from the others was into the mysterious
and frightening confines of the forest. They discovered shortly
that the deeper into the woods they went, the more lost and
confused they became. The Eagle and his companions couldn't
even agree on which way to turn. (*They begin bumping into one
another.*)

Bee:
Which way should we go?

All:
This way! (*Each points in a different direction.*)

Eagle:
Well, who needs you?

All:
Who needs you? (*They all set off in their own direction.*)

Narrator:
The further each one went on his or her own, the more desperate
and lost each became. (*Each animal freezes in fear.*)
     Mother Nature returned to the Meadow to see how her
animal family was getting along. She was troubled when Spider
told her the story of how Eagle and the others had set off in the
forest by themselves.

Skunk:
I'm worried, Mother Nature. What will happen to them? And
what will become of our family?

Mother:
Listen. (*Mother Nature hears something.*)

Monkey:
I can't hear anything.

Owl:
Try again, only this time listen with your heart. (*They all listen intently. Eagle and the others are frozen. They don't move lips but their voices are heard on tape pleading: "Help me! Help me! Please, help me!"*)

Skunk:
I can't stand it. Make them stop! Make it go away! (*Skunk starts to cover her ears.*)

Owl:
Once you've listened with your heart, Skunk, you can't pretend that you don't hear their cries.

Turtle:
Listen to me. Don't go looking for trouble. Let's count our blessings. They didn't need us. It serves them right! So what do you want? We should follow them and then we will all be lost forever in those woods?

Mother:
You need them, Turtle, just as they need you. Alone you can never hope to become a real family. They will never find their way out of the forest by themselves. Even now they are each separated from each other and frighteningly alone.

Monkey:
They didn't seem to need us before.

Owl:
Perhaps they were just blind to their need of us as we can be blind to our need of them.

Turtle:
Do you mind putting that in a simple sentence, Owl?

Mother:
The Owl's right. You need each other. Eagle and the others need

you to teach them the values of the heart. Only you can teach them how to become vulnerable and intimate and committed. And you need them to share your joys and sorrows, your laughter and tears, to listen to your stories, to respond to your touch . . .

Skunk:
To become a REAL family.

Mother:
That's right.

Monkey:
Well, they couldn't do it before. What makes you so sure they could or would now?

Spider:
Mother Nature is right, Monkey. What do my stories take?

Monkey:
Time. Lots of time.

Spider:
And what does becoming a family take?

Skunk:
Time. Lots of time.

Spider:
It took us time to learn how to depend on one another, to share with each other, to tell our stories, to laugh and play, to listen with the heart. It will take Eagle and the others time. But without them we will never be a whole family. We can't do without them any more than they can do without us.

Narrator:
And so, Spider and the others huddled together and faced the unknown dangers lurking in the forest. They were not even sure they could find the others. All they knew was that they must, at

least, try. Slowly they made their way into the woods. They listened long and hard to the cries of the others. It led them first to the Ostrich who was hiding under his pail. The Ostrich was so happy to be found that he joyfully embraced the Skunk. The little band continued and, next, came upon the Squirrel who was stuck inside of a tree because of all the nuts he had gathered and was unwilling to let go of. Turtle gradually got Squirrel to give enough of them up to be free of the tree. The Turtle extended a hand to Squirrel in friendship and welcome. Squirrel was so happy to be found that he gave everyone all the nuts he or she could eat.

As the group moved further into the forest they came upon Peacock. She was exhausted, frightened and a general mess. When the Owl put a reassuring hand on her shoulder, she covered her face in embarrassment. Owl and the others embraced her and welcomed her warmly. And she, too, was happy to be found . . . even if her feathers were ruffled and wilted.

They next happened upon Bee. She was so tired from spelling out her cries for H-E-L-P, Help! that she was ready to collapse. Tears of joy came to her eyes as the band of animals slowly appeared.

Monkey:
What do you feel now, Bee?

Bee:
Relief.

Monkey:
And how do you spell relief?

Bee:
I spell it, F-O-U-N-D, Found!

Narrator:
As the animals moved deeper into the forest, they finally came upon the Eagle. He, too, had obviously been crying and was embarrassed to have the other animals see him this way. Know-

ing that the best defense is a strong offense, he spoke before the others had a chance.

Eagle:
Well, lucky for you that I happened upon you. Are you all lost?

Spider:
That's funny, we were about to ask you the same question. Will you join us?

Eagle:
I'm not lost! I don't need you, any of you. I'm doing quite well by myself.

Squirrel:
Well, none of us are.

Bee:
We can either wander alone or wander together.

Ostrich:
I want to do it together!

Owl:
Besides, Eagle, we know you need us, even if you find that hard to admit. And we want you to know that we need you and your gifts.

Skunk:
Please come with us. We'll never be a whole family without you.

Eagle:
(*Embarrassed*) Ohhhhh . . . all right!

Narrator:
Then the little family of animals began to celebrate, for they were all together again.

Eagle:
Hey, wait a minute. We're all together now. But how do we get out of the forest.

Spider:
Yeah, what'll we do?

Mother:
(*Mother Nature appears in the forest*) Remember, my little friends, that you now have one another.

Owl:
But how do we get out of the forest?

Mother:
The only way out of the forest is by going deeper into it.

Bee:
But that doesn't make any sense, S-E-N-S-E, sense!

Monkey:
I know, but Mother Nature has never led us astray. (*Recorded cries of "Help us! Help us! Please, help us!" are heard.*)

Peacock:
What did you say?

Owl:
Nothing.

Skunk:
Then who was that crying out?

Turtle:
Shhhh! For crying out loud, listen! (*The cries continue.*)

Bee:
(*Obviously counting heads*) Well, we're all here, H-E-R-E, here!

Peacock:
It must be a pigment of our imagination.

Eagle:
Yeah, something that happens to animals who are lost for any
length of time . . . like all of you!

Ostrich:
No, my friends, those are cries for help.

Squirrel:
But how can you hear them?

Ostrich:
Because I used to cry it out myself.

Eagle:
But I can't hear it.

Ostrich:
You can only hear it if you listen with your heart. That's what
this experience and our friends have taught us.

Monkey:
What'll we do?

Spider:
Look for them.

Eagle:
Look for them! But why?

Ostrich:
Because they, like us, need to be found.

Narrator:
And so, the timid little family of animals began wading further
into the mysterious depths of the forest. They were united in
their need for one another and their desire to seek out the lost . . .

those whose cries they could only hear with their hearts. (*Mother Nature watches them move out. She smiles. The animals move toward the congregation. They look out over them, long and hard, from left to right, searching.*)

Finis

Lost and Found

Theme:
Community.

Props:
  (1) Recorded music as Mother Nature and meadow theme. An appropriate selection from Rossini's "Guillaume Tell" is suggested.
  (2) Recorded music as Forest and imminent danger theme. An appropriate selection from Rossini's "Guillaume Tell" is suggested.
  (3) Recorded thunder clap.
  (4) Recorded cries for help.
  (5) One wand for Mother Nature.
  (6) One aviator's hat and goggles for the Eagle.
  (7) One yellow striped shirt for the Bee.
  (8) One handled mirror for the Peacock.
  (9) One pail held by the Ostrich and frequently put over his head.
  (10) One brown turtleneck shirt for the Monkey.
  (11) One bicycle helmet for the Turtle.
  (12) Knitting needles and yarn for the Spider.
  (13) One pair of dark glasses and one cane for the Owl.
  (14) One clothes pin.
  (15) One atomizer for the Skunk.
  (16) One black turtleneck shirt for the Skunk.
  (17) One whistle for Mother Nature.
  (18) One camera with which to take a family picture.
  (19) One tray of nuts for the Squirrel.

Production Notes:

A word of encouragement and a reminder are in order. Don't be imprisoned by the list of suggested props and music. Make your own adaptations, simplifications or embellishments where it seems appropriate for you. These items are listed after every story drama simply to let you know what was used in the original telling of these stories.

When the two groups of animals are reunited toward the end of this storydrama, they once again hear cries for help. All the animals should look in the direction of the congregation. When the animals begin to move out, they move in the direction of the congregation.

Study Questions

(1) In your imagination, become the Lost Sheep. Experience what life was like with the flock and the Shepherd. How did you get lost? What were your thoughts, what were your feelings, and what were your body sensations while you were lost? What did you experience when you first heard the Shepherd's voice? What did you hear in his/her voice? What did you experience when you were reunited with the flock?

(2) Identify with the Lost Sheep. What parts of your life (past/present/future) are called up? What parts of yourself or your life does the Lost Sheep symbolize? Have a dialogue with the Lost Sheep. Ask the Lost Sheep to tell you what it was like being lost. Ask the Lost Sheep what thoughts, feelings and body sensations it had while it was lost. Ask the Lost Sheep to give you his/her impressions of you. Can the Lost Sheep detect or reveal some forgotten or lost part of you or your experience? Ask the Lost Sheep what he/she learned from this whole experience. What happened to the Lost Sheep after this experience? What advice or wisdom can the Lost Sheep share with you?

(3) In your imagination, become the Shepherd. Dwell in the Shepherd's acts. What are your thoughts, feelings, and body

sensations throughout this experience? How does this experience change you? What do you learn from this experience? What if the parable ended with your not finding the Lost Sheep? What would you experience in this case? As Shepherd, become aware of some part of yourself that is lost or forgotten. Go in search of part of yourself. What do you experience? What do you find? Now become the Shepherd who is searching for something lost outside of yourself. Who or what is this? What do you find? How do these experiences change you? What do you learn?

(4) Try this exercise in your journal. Focus on the four key words of this parable: [1] losing, [2] seeking, [3] finding, and [4] rejoicing. Begin with the word "losing." Write down all the experiences of losing or loss that you have had. What are some of the things that you have lost? Adapt and do this exercise with each of the key words. Use your imagination and create a story that captures in a different way the experiences of losing, seeking, finding and rejoicing.

(5) Sometimes you can learn things about yourself by means of association and identification. In your journal, write down your answers to the following questions. If you were any animal in the world, what animal would you be? Why would you be that animal? What do you like about that animal? In the story drama, which animal did you like most? What did you like about this animal? Explain. Which animal did you like least? What didn't you like about this animal? Explain. Did you identify with any animal in the story drama? Which one did you identify with? Explain. Think about your parents. If you could pick any animals in the world to capture them (describe them to us), what animals would they be? Explain. What animals would your brothers and sisters be? Explain. Do this exercise with a friend. Each of you write down what animal you think you would be. Also write down what animal you think your friend would be. Share and explain your selections.

(6) What does Mother Nature want all of the animals to do? What is their response? What are the most satisfying aspects of being a part of a family or community? Write these down in your

journal. What are the most difficult aspects of being a part of a family or community? Do you find it easier to pick out what you like or dislike in others? Here is a family or community exercise. Sit in a circle so that you can see one another. Read 1 Corinthians 12:4–11. After hearing this reading, spend some time thinking about the different gifts that you have experienced in your family or community. What gifts have most helped you? Some gifts might be: understanding, encouragement, forgiveness, laughter, care, tears, tenderness, and so on. When everyone has had a chance to reflect, someone begins by standing up and mentioning one gift he or she has experienced in this family or community. He or she remains standing. If someone else hears the gift he or she was going to mention, that person simply stands. When everyone is standing, conclude by singing a doxology or praying: "Good and gracious God, we give you thanks for these and all your gifts which we have experienced because you love us through Christ our Lord. Amen."

(7) What does the meadow symbolize for you? What does the forest symbolize for you? What happens to Eagle and the animals when they go into the forest? Why does this happen to them? Have you ever thought, like Eagle, that you don't need anybody else? Why or why not? Explain. What do Spider and the other animals do? Why do they go looking for Eagle and the animals lost in the forest? What happens when they are all reunited? Who else is lost in the forest? What are some of the cries for help that you hear in your life? Write in your journal what some of those cries for help would be outside of you as well as inside of you.

(8) What words would you use to describe Eagle and the animals that set off on their own? What words would you use to describe Spider and those animals that went looking for them? Of all the words that you have listed, which ones describe you? Why do these words describe you? How are these two groups of animals parts of a whole? Why do they need each other? What do they possibly have to give to one another? Explain. Have you ever heard of Jean Vanier and the community with the handicapped called *L'Arche* that he founded in Trosly-Bruiel, France? Explore and discover what this man and his communities are all about.

Get one of Vanier's books, *Be Not Afraid* or *Community and Growth,* or the book *Enough Room for Joy* by Bill Clarke which describes Vanier's vision and work. What can you learn about building, sustaining and living community from Jean Vanier and *L'Arche?*

11. Martha and Mary

(Luke 10:38–42)

On their journey Jesus entered a village where a woman named Martha welcomed him to her home. She had a sister named Mary, who seated herself at the Lord's feet and listened to his words. Martha, who was busy with all the details of hospitality, came to him and said, "Lord, are you not concerned that my sister has left me to do the household tasks all alone? Tell her to help me."

The Lord in reply said to her: "Martha, Martha, you are anxious and upset about many things; one thing only is required. Mary has chosen the better portion and she shall not be deprived of it."

The Road to Bethany

Cast:

The Narrator	Giuseppe
Lilly (the Director)	Genesius
Dympna	Cecilia
Gomer	Juliana Irabug
Louise	Gaston LePlus
Simon	Loreta Spes
Zita	Odo

Narrator:

Once upon a time, in the early days of the Kingdom, an annual drama competition was held to bring all of the cities of the Kingdom together. This drama festival was better than the competitions of early Greece. The plays that were performed at it would literally knock your sarx off.

The city of Diver decided to enter the competition this particular year. They formed a Drama Guild just for this purpose. Every citizen of Diver was automatically a member of the Guild. Under the supervision of . . . well, *no one* and *everyone,* the citizens were gearing up for the competition. They decided to stage a production of an ancient story from their collection of sacred legends. Their play was entitled *The Road to Bethany.*

The inhabitants of Diver participated in the production in one of two ways. Certain citizens had roles in the play. They acted. The other citizens contributed technical assistance as members of the stagecrew. These people built sets, made costumes, ran the lights and attended to the thousand little details that are part of any dramatic production. (*Gomer carries a small potted plant across the stage. Each time he carries it the plant will be bigger.*)

However, things were not going well for the little Drama

209

Guild. Tensions mounted. Misunderstandings compounded. And tempers were running high.

Zita:

Tempers! Tempers! Get your tempers here! Fifty cents each or two for a dollar.

Narrator:

Those who were acting thought that the stagecrew was contributing nothing to the production. In fact, the actors believed that the stagecrew just made a horribly confusing racket which distracted them from the task at hand. (*The noises of hammers and saws make it difficult for the actors to hear one another and concentrate. The actors try to do their lines but to no avail. Finally, they all put their hands on their hips and glare at the stagecrew.*)

On the other hand (*the stagecrew all do one-handed demonstrative gesture*), the stagecrew thought that the actors contributed nothing valuable to the production. They only got in the way of the real work that had to be done.

Odo:

(*Trying to read from his play book*) She was busy with all the details of hospitality. (*Hammer noise begins.*) So she came to him and said:

Loreta:

(*Loreta tries to go to Gaston but Giuseppe and Dympna carry a piece of lumber between her and Gaston. Giuseppe and Dympna are in carpenter overalls with derby hats and black ties on. They do a Laurel and Hardy routine with the board. While Loreta successfully ducks twice, she receives a swat the third time.*) Aren't you concerned (*she ducks*) that my sister has left me to do all the work alone? (*she ducks*) Tell her to help me. (*She smiles and then gets hit.*) Ooooowwwww!!!

Gaston:

(*Reading from his play book*) You're anxious and upset about many things.

Loreta:
You would be, too, if it were you they were trying to kill!

Genesius:
Just pretend they are not here! (*Gomer walks across stage with the potted plant. It is bigger.*)

Loreta:
I'm beginning to wonder whether we'll survive this production.

Zita:
How dramatic!

Louise:
You know something, Zita, that's the first believable line she's spoken the entire rehearsal! (*Louise applauds Loreta and then the other members of the stagecrew follow suit. Loreta pouts!*)

Narrator:
There was no way that Diver's dramatic production would be ready for the competition if things continued to degenerate. So, Gaston LePlus took things into his own hands. (*Gaston starts picking up every object he can get his hands on*) . . . ahem! I mean, he went out and hired a director. (Gaston drops everything and goes to escort Lilly onto the stage.) He hoped she might bring some order out of all this chaos. Her name was Lilly.

When she arrived, everyone in the Guild was excited. The stagecrew took her luggage and showed her set designs, lighting charts and completed costumes.

Simon:
We sure are glad you're here, Miss Lilly.

Gomer:
(*Gomer is walking across the stage with the potted plant. It has grown again.*) Yeah, maybe now we'll get something done! (*All the stagecrew rub their hands in anticipation of getting to work.*)

Narrator:
The actors were pleased that Lilly had come. They gave her a chair and all sat around her feet. They wanted to spend their time talking with her. They shared their insights, hopes and dreams for this dramatic production. They listened to her. They hung on her every word and thoroughly enjoyed her presence.

The stagecrew was equally pleased at her arrival. They worked extra hard so that the lights, the costumes and the scenery would be perfect. Soon, however, the stagecrew realized that while they were all busily preparing the technical parts of the production, the actors were just sitting around Lilly doing nothing but listening to her.

Lilly:
I think you'd have more understanding for Juliana's character if you used the method I suggested. Try walking a mile in her shoes.

Actors:
Ooooohhhh!

Juliana:
But how do we do that, Lilly?

Lilly:
I believe it's Lao-tzu who said that a journey of three thousand miles is begun by a single step.

Actors:
Aaaaahhhh!

Stagecrew:
Tthhpphhhh! (*Raspberry noise is directed toward Lilly and the actors.*)

Narrator:
The stagecrew continued to grumble (*they all voice "grumble" a number of times*) and murmur (*they all voice "murmur" a number of times*). Finally, they came to Lilly and complained.

Lilly:
And what exactly bothers you about the actors?

Simon:
They have a bad attitude.

Louise:
The thoughts and feelings they express are not their own.

Zita:
Yeah! You can't trust them or their expressions.

Gomer:
(*He comes in carrying the potted plant which has grown again.*)
Besides, they're not doing anything to help the play along.

Gaston:
And who are you to criticize us?

Cecilia:
We are the ones whom the people will see!

Odo:
We're the ones who will win this competition!

Crew:
Oh yeah?

Actors:
Yeah!

Narrator:
Lilly realized that she had to do something dramatic in order to get the Guild working together again.

Lilly:
All right folks, I've got an idea. I think we've been going about this production entirely the wrong way.

Narrator:
And so, Lilly began reassigning parts and responsibilities. She
gave the acting roles to all the stagecrew and the technical jobs to
all the actors. Both groups grumbled at first. (*They all voice
"grumble" a number of times in unison.*) But Lilly insisted that
only if they changed parts would the play ever be presented.
Because they all wanted the play to work, they accepted their
new roles. So rehearsals resumed again.

Lilly:
Louise and Zita, the audience will never hear you if you speak
your lines with your backs to them. (*They turn around and are
self-conscious.*) All right, Louise, you love Simon. You hang on
his every word. (*They try this but it only comes out humorously.*)

Juliana:
She looks like a drooling dog!

Loreta:
More like a sick cow!

Gaston:
Pardon me, Lilly. Are you playing it as a comedy now? (*Lilly just
looks at him.*)

Odo:
This is the way we hammer the nails. (*Odo hits his thumb.*)
Ooowww!

Simon:
You mean, this is the way you hit your thumb!

Genesius:
Where should I put this, Gaston? (*Genesius hits Juliana in the
stomach with the board he is carrying.*)

Juliana:
Ooowww!

Gaston:
No! No! The other way! (*Genesius turns the other way and hits Loreta in the butt.*)

Loreta:
Ouch! Hey, Bimbo, watch where you're going!

Genesius:
The name's Genesius, Loreta.

Gomer:
(*He walks across the stage with the potted plant bigger.*) Genesius is the name. Ineptitude's the game!

Genesius:
So you thought it would be easy doing our job, did you?

Dympna:
Let that be a lesson to you!

Narrator:
Things were going from bad to worse. Everything was becoming more frustrating and more confused. Suddenly all the theatre lights went out.

Gaston:
Oh no! What happened now?

Giuseppe:
I think you blew a fuse!

Dympna:
Yes, indeed, a fuse!

Giuseppe:
Would you be quiet? I already said that! (*Dympna scratches her head and begins whining in Stan Laurel fashion.*)

Actors:
Help! (*Plaintively.*)

Stagecrew:
What do we do now?

Lilly:
(*She lights a big match and gives it to Giuseppe.*) Here Giuseppe. Do you know where a flashlight is?

Giuseppe:
Yes, Miss Lilly.

Dympna:
Indeed he does!

Giuseppe:
Would you be quiet? (*Dympna turns to person behind her with forefinger over mouth indicating "shhhhhhhh."*)

Lilly:
Then get it and go help Loreta with the lights. (*Giuseppe takes the match from Lilly, goes over and gives it to Loreta. With Loreta holding the match, Giuseppe takes out a flashlight, changes the fuse and the lights come back on. All sigh in relief.*) O.K., folks, coffee break's over. Back to work. (*They all start to slowly go back to their jobs. Something is different.*)

Narrator:
And so all the members of the Guild began applying themselves once again to their new jobs.

Zita:
(*Reading from the play book*) Aren't you concerned that my sister has left me to do all the work?

Gaston:
(*He comes over and gently turns Zita around.*) Remember, Zita, don't speak with your back to the audience.

Zita:
Listen, you people can do this better than I can. Honestly! Loreta, this is your role, not mine. (*Lilly begins to smile.*) You play it. It was meant for you.

Genesius:
And our doing the technical jobs is a joke! You'll be lucky if we don't destroy the whole place.

Loreta:
(*To Giuseppe and Dympna*) Yeah! You two know this job better than I do. I don't know a right fuse from a wrong fuse.

Dympna:
That's because two heads are better than one! Right, Giuseppe?

Giuseppe:
I couldn't have said it better, Dympna!

Narrator:
So, slowly each member of the Guild went back to his or her original role or task. Everyone was surprised that Lilly had no objections. Finally Gaston spoke up.

Gaston:
Lilly, I thought you said that for this play to work we had to change parts.

Lilly:
That's right, Gaston. But you have to change parts in your hearts. You all needed to understand and appreciate the roles and tasks that were not your own.

All:
Oooooohhhhhhh!!! (*Nodding heads.*)

Narrator:
The Guild was so impressed with Lilly's wisdom and so pleased with her ability to help them all work together that they made

her the first honorary member of their Guild. Thus she became the first Guilded Lilly in the city of Diver. (*Gomer carries out a potted lily that has been spray painted gold and gives it to Lilly.*)

Not only did the Guild win the drama competition, but, more importantly, they all discovered unity in Diver city.

Finis

The Road to Bethany

Theme:
Unity.

Props:
(1) Six potted plants. The first plant is very small. The sixth plant is very tall. The other plants are of gradually increased growth.
(2) One hammer.
(3) One long 2 × 4 piece of lumber.
(4) Two pairs of carpenter overalls for Giuseppe and Dympna.
(5) Two black derby hats for Giuseppe and Dympna.
(6) Two long sleeve white shirts and black ties for Giuseppe and Dympna.
(7) Three play books or scripts.
(8) One potted lilly spray painted gold.
(9) One flash light.
(10) One stick match and stick match box.

Production Notes:
A number of classic comic routines can be used in this story drama. Giuseppe and Dympna are patterned after the comedy team of Laurel and Hardy.

One of those classic routines is that of the plant that becomes larger every time it is carried across the stage. That is why Gomer will need six potted plants of varying sizes. These can be made out of cardboard or other materials. They don't have to be genuine plants.

Study Questions:

(1) Eugene Laverdiere, in his book *The New Testament in the Life of the Church* (Notre Dame: Ave Maria Press, 1980), explores the meaning of the questions that we bring to a story. He contends that the process that he outlines produces the best results when it is employed as a group effort in which the participants share their observations and help one another discern what is truly in the story. In your study group, read the story of Martha and Mary (Luke 10:38–42).

Next, as a group, ask the following questions of this story: [1] *Where?* Where does the action or event take place? [2] *When?* When does the action or event take place? [3] *Who?* Who are the characters involved in the story? List all the participants. Note how the characters are introduced and described. Ask who is the principal character. [4] *What?* What happens in the story? [5] *How?* How is the story told? What role does the narrator play? How does the dialogue or discourse contribute to the story? How are the names, titles, special terms and language in general used? [6] *Why?* Why does the author share this story with the readers? What are some of the insights that you discover by asking these six questions of this scriptural story?

(2) What do the characters Martha, Mary and Jesus symbolize for you? Write down the strengths and weaknesses, what you like and dislike about each of these characters. Which character do you identify with most? Why? Which character do you identify with least? Why? In your journal, write down the answers to the following questions: Who is the Martha in you? Who is the Mary in you? Who is the Jesus in you?

(3) Spend some time with each of the characters in this story. Dialogue with each of them. Ask them any questions that you have ever wanted to ask them. What are their replies? Before you leave each character, ask them if there is anything that they would like to tell you. It could be some piece of wisdom that they wish to share with you that might help you in the living of your

life. What do they tell you? This exercise may be made easier by writing out the dialogue in your journal.

(4) Jesus tells Martha that she is anxious about many things. Are you anxious about many things? On a piece of paper or in your journal, list what you are anxious about. Keep asking yourself: "What am I anxious about?" Write down the first thing that comes to mind. Then repeat the question to yourself again. Go for as long as you can. Then reread this scriptural story holding your list of anxieties in your hands. What are your thoughts, feelings, and body sensations as you experience the story this time?

(5) Jesus tells Martha: "You are anxious and upset about many things. Only one thing is necessary." Reflect on these words of Jesus. Hear them addressed to you. Then, in your journal, write down what the one thing is that is necessary for you.

(6) Have you ever seen Steve Allen's television show "The Meeting of the Minds"? On this show four characters from different epochs of history come together to discuss various topics. Imagine a session of "The Meeting of the Minds" with Martha, Mary, Jesus and yourself. You can be the moderator and direct the discussion. What do you discuss with these characters? What questions do you ask? How do the characters respond to you, your questions, one another and one another's responses? What do you learn about them? What do you learn about yourself?

(7) In the story drama, what did those who acted think about the stagecrew? What did the stagecrew think about those members of Diver city who acted? Why does Gaston LePlus hire a director? Who is she? What happens when she arrives? Why were the actors pleased that Lilly had come? What did they do? Why were the stagecrew happy about Lilly's arrival? What did they do? What did the stagecrew murmur and grumble about? Why does Lilly reassign parts and responsibilities? What happens?

(8) What happens when the lights go out? How are they turned back on? Who are the people in your life who have given you

light or been light for you when you felt the lights had gone off? How were these people light for you? Who are some of the people in your life who have called good or gifts out of you that you did not know existed? How did they do this for you? How can you do this for others? Write down some of the ways in your journal. Do you find it easy or difficult to see, to appreciate and to affirm the gifts of others? Why? For the period of a week, spend some time each evening reflecting on how affirming you were of other people and their gifts. Make a deliberate effort to affirm the good in yourself and in those around you. Look for it. Explore ways you might be able to do this. What is the transformation that occurs for the cast and crew? How does it come about? Think of some people you don't appreciate. What don't you like about them? Try to put yourself in their shoes. What do you experience? Discuss the ways you can discover unity in diversity.

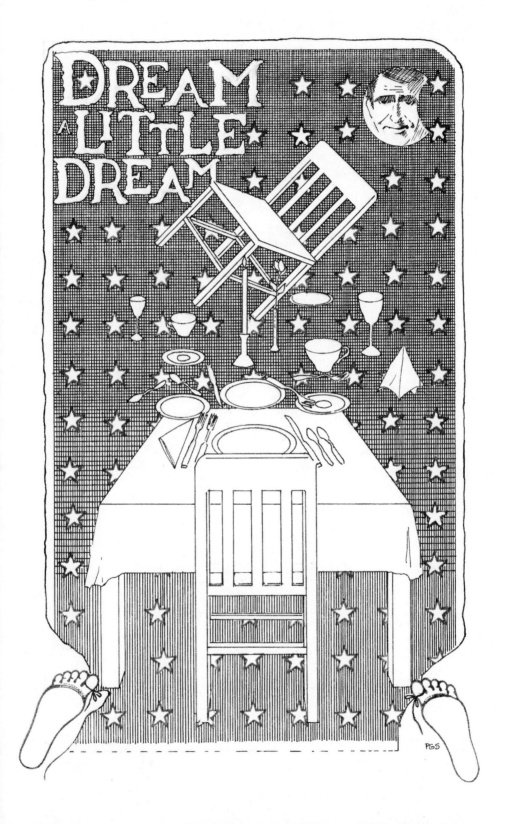

12. Dives and Lazarus

(Luke 16:19–31)

"Once there was a rich man who dressed in purple and linen and feasted splendidly every day. At his gate lay a beggar named Lazarus who was covered with sores. Lazarus longed to eat the scraps that fell from the rich man's table. The dogs even came and licked his sores. Eventually, the beggar died. He was carried by angels to the bosom of Abraham. The rich man likewise died and was buried. From the abode of the dead where he was in torment, he raised his eyes and saw Abraham afar off, and Lazarus resting in his bosom.

"He called out, 'Father Abraham, have pity on me. Send Lazarus to dip the tip of his finger in water to refresh my tongue, for I am tormented in these flames.' 'My child,' replied Abraham, 'remember that you were well off in your lifetime, while Lazarus was in misery. Now he has found consolation here, but you have found torment. And that is not all. Between you and us there is fixed a great abyss, so that those who might wish to cross from here to you cannot do so, nor can anyone cross from your side to us.'

" 'Father, I ask you then,' the rich man said, 'send him to my father's house where I have five brothers. Let him be a warning to them so that they may not end in this place of torment.' Abraham answered, 'They have Moses and the prophets. Let them hear them.' 'No, Father Abraham,' replied the rich man. 'But if someone would only go to them from the dead, they would repent.' Abraham said to him, 'If they do not listen to Moses and the prophets, they will not be convinced even if one should rise from the dead. ' "

Dream a Little Dream

Cast:

Narrator

Barnabas B. Bags

Eustice I. Fleecem

Maitre d'

Waiter

Bus Boy

Sandman

Constable

Dream-Person Bags

Dream-Person Eustice

Tramp-1

Tramp-2

Tramp-3

Narrator:

[*The scene is set as the music begins. The theme music is from The Twilight Zone. An aristocrat (Eustice) is in a restaurant eating a sumptuous meal. Bags and friends look in the window of the restaurant longingly. They all freeze as the Twilight Zone music comes up again.*]

You unlock this story with the key of imagination. Beyond it is another dimension. A dimension of new sounds. A dimension of new sights. A dimension of new thoughts and feelings. At the restaurant up ahead, the next stop is the TWILIGHT ZONE.

Eustice:

Garcon? (*Eustice snaps fingers to get the Waiter's attention.*) Garcon!

Waiter:

Yes, Monsieur?

Eustice:

That lobster tail was such a tender morsel, I think I'll have six more.

Waiter:
Only six? Would Monsieur like anything else with that? Perhaps a feather? Or maybe another bottle of our finest Muscatel?

Eustice:
That's an excellent idea! But this time, don't try to rotate your old stock on me. Bring me a bottle of your finest *Vino Nouveau*. (*The Waiter leaves and the Bus Boy takes the plates.*)

Tramp-1:
That was the finest meal I've ever seen.

Tramp-2:
I couldn't watch him eat another bite, I'm so full.

Tramp-3:
(*Burps*) I watched too much myself. (*Tramp-3 pulls out toothpicks and gives them out.*)

Waiter:
Here you are, Monsieur. Six lobster tails and one bottle of wine.

Eustice:
I've changed my mind. Just put them on my bill. I'm ready to go.

Bus Boy:
(*To the Waiter*) If I ate that much, I'd be ready to go too!

Waiter:
Would Monsieur like me to put this in a doggy bag?

Eustice:
Don't bother. Just throw it away! (*Eustice gets up.*)

Bags:
Look! All of that's just going to waste!

Tramp-1:
Don't do anything foolish, Bags.

Bags:
I'm going to get us those leftovers. (*Bags moves to the restaurant door. Eustice takes out his wallet and pays the Maitre d'. Eustice starts out the restaurant door with wallet in hand. Eustice collides with Bags. The wallet drops to the floor. Bags picks up the wallet and goes to return it to Eustice.*)

Eustice:
Help! Help! I've been robbed! (*The Maitre d' and the Waiter come outside.*)

Bags:
No you haven't. You just dropped your wallet. Here!

Eustice:
Dropped it, my eye! You stole it! Maitre d', get the Constable.

Maitre d':
(*To the Waiter*) Waiter, get the Constable.

Waiter:
(*To the Bus Boy*) Pardon me, boy, would you get the Constable?

Bus Boy:
(*To no one*) Go get the Consta . . . (*The Bus Boy realizes there is no one and so he goes and gets the Constable.*)

Bags:
Wait a minute! Wait a minute! You're making a big mistake. This was all an accident.

Eustice:
There's no such thing as an accident! (*The Constable comes in.*) Constable, get this low-life out of my sight! (*The Constable grabs Bags. Bags resists. Eustice turns his back on Bags. Eustice starts to walk away. Bags, held by the Constable, reaches out pleadingly towards Eustice. All the characters freeze.*)

Narrator:
Meet Barnabas B. Bags. "Bags" to his friends. Tramp. Vagrant. To some, a low-life. A man of perplexing paradox. Gold on the inside but rust on the outside. And over here is Eustice I. Fleecem. A man of very different composition. Two people living in two different worlds. Or are they?

Their fates are inexorably bound. This evening they will both be given the opportunity to experience the refining fire of dreams. Though they have met only briefly, they will meet again in . . . THE TWILIGHT ZONE.

Constable:
(*The Narrator exits. All the other characters come to life.*) All right, now, that'll be enough of these shenanigans. All of youse get out of here. It's late. Go home and go to bed!

Tramp-2:
Well, sweet dreams, officer.

Constable:
And the same to all of youse. (*They all exit. On stage left, Bags goes home and gets ready for bed. On stage right, Eustice goes home and gets ready for bed. They both put on nightgowns and caps. Bags' gown and hat have holes in them.*)

Sandman:
(*The three Tramps hold cut-outs of the STARS, MOON, and CLOUDS on sticks over Bags. The Maitre d', the Waiter and the Bus Boy do it for Eustice. These symbolize sleep and dreams. Bags and Eustice go to sleep. The Sandman enters. The Sandman ties the big toes of Bags and Eustice together with a piece of yarn. Then the Sandman sprinkles fairy dust over Bags who begins to dream. Bags' dream comes to life. In both Bags' dream and Eustice's dream, the real Bags and Eustice remain sleeping. Their Dream-Person characters act out the dreams.*)

Bags:
[*The dream sequence for Bags is done in mime. All the characters, in dreamlike walks, assume their positions inside and outside the*

restaurant. *Eustice walks out the restaurant door with his wallet in his hand. The Maitre d', the Waiter and the Bus Boy look out the window at him. They wave. Eustice waves back. As Eustice is waving, Bags bumps into him. Eustice drops his wallet but doesn't notice this. Eustice leaves. Bags joins the restaurant crew in waving "good-bye" to Eustice.*

The Restaurant crew point down at the street. Bags is confused. Bags starts dancing to entertain them. They laugh and shake their heads "No." They point down at the sidewalk again. Bags looks down and sees the wallet filled with money. He picks it up and looks at the people in the restaurant. They applaud him.

Bags gathers the three Tramps and takes them all into the restaurant for a meal. They sit down. The Maitre d', the Waiter and the Bus Boy serve them. When the food and drink are brought, Bags insists that the restaurant crew sit down at table and share the meal with the Tramps and himself.

While they are feasting, Eustice comes back to the restaurant disheveled. He has no money. He is hungry and lost. He looks into the restaurant window longingly at Bags and friends. The Maitre d' notices Eustice and starts pointing to him and laughing. All of the characters begin laughing at him except Bags. Bags looks at him in his misery. Bags gets up from table and goes outside to Eustice. Bags brings Eustice into the restaurant with him. Bags sits Eustice down in his own chair. All the characters welcome Eustice and share the meal with him.

Bags gives Eustice his wallet back. The others look apprehensive about this. Eustice takes out lots of money and gives it to the Maitre d' with a broad gesture that it is for everyone. All are relieved. Eustice gets up and embraces Bags. All rejoice. Then all of the characters move in dreamlike walks back to their original positions.]

Sandman:
(*Comes out and sprinkles dust on Eustice. Bags sleeps blissfully. Eustice begins tossing and turning. All the characters move in a dreamlike manner to their new positions. The Maitre d', the Waiter and the Bus Boy are in the restaurant. The three Tramps are seated in the restaurant. Bags and Eustice go to the door of the restaurant.*)

D-P Eustice:
Where do you think you're going?

D-P Bags:
To dine, perchance to feast.

D-P Eustice:
They won't let you in there dressed like that!

D-P Bags:
Au contraire, mon ami, they won't let you in there dressed like that. (*Both go to the restaurant door and are met by the Maitre d'.*)

Maitre d':
So good to see you, Monsieur.

D-P Bags:
Thank you.

D-P Eustice:
Thank you.

Maitre d':
Your regular table, Monsieur?

D-P Bags:
But of course!

D-P Eustice:
But of course!

Maitre d':
This way, Monsieur. (*Both Bags and Eustice start to follow the Maitre d'. The Maitre d' notices Eustice following and speaks to him.*) And where do you think you are going?

D-P Eustice:
To my regular table.

Maitre d':
Oh, I see. Monsieur has a little joke with me. However, that is impossible! This is Monsieur Bags' table.

D-P Eustice:
That's impossible! That's my table. It's always been my table.

D-P Bags:
You must be dreaming, my good man. They don't serve low-lifes like you in here. (*The Tramps and staff join Bags in a good laugh at Eustice.*)

D-P Eustice:
Wait a minute! Wait a minute! What's going on?

Maitre d':
Please, sir, you're making a scene. Just leave quietly and there will be no more trouble.

D-P Bags:
I'm quickly losing my appetite. Can't you call the Constable to deal with this?

Maitre d':
(*To the Waiter*) Garcon, call the Constable!

Waiter:
(*To the Bus Boy*) Boy, call the Constable!

Bus Boy:
(*To Eustice*) Hey, you! Call the Constable, will you?

D-P Eustice:
(*Angrily*) You bet I will! (*Eustice goes to the door of the restaurant and yells.*) Help! Help! (*Eustice returns to the table. The Constable comes in.*)

Constable:
What seems to be the matter? (*They all look and gesture to*

Eustice.) Now what's a low-life like you doing in a nice place like
this?

D-P Eustice:
(*Dumbfounded*) Well, I . . . I . . .

D-P Bags:
Officer, would you please remove this nuisance so we can eat in
peace?

Constable:
Yes sir, Mr. Bags. I apologize for the inconvenience. I can assure
you that it won't happen again. (*The Constable starts to drag
Eustice out of the restaurant. As the Constable and Eustice go by
the restaurant window, they pause. Eustice looks in at Bags. Bags
looks back at him and then orders dinner from the Waiter.*)

Waiter:
And what is Monsieur Bags' pleasure this evening?

D-P Bags:
How about six of your tenderest lobster tails and a bottle of your
finest Muscatel. (*All the characters freeze. They return to their
places in dream-like walks. When all of the characters have exited
except the real Bags and Eustice, these two slowly wake up. As they
come to consciousness, they both notice the yarn tied to their big
toes. Bags and Eustice untie their toes and then begin following the
yarn. When they meet in the center they are startled. They look at
each other, then out to the congregation. They freeze.*)

Narrator:
A restaurant. A wallet. A chance encounter. The stuff of dreams.
For some, they hold no significance. But for those who are able
to see and hear, they are the stuff of transformation.

Two people have met. Two worlds have collided. Have their
waking and dreaming encounters changed them? The answer to
that can only be found by entering. . . .THE TWILIGHT ZONE.

Finis

Dream a Little Dream

Theme:
Conversion.

Props:
(1) Twilight Zone theme recorded from the television program or from the Manhattan Transfer's album *Extensions.*
(2) One recording of "Mr. Sandman" from the album *The Best of Vaughn Monroe.*
(3) Four chairs.
(4) One large standing frame of a window.
(5) One dark jacket, pair of pants, white shirt and tie for Maitre d'.
(6) One red vest, white shirt and dark bow tie for Waiter.
(7) One white towel for Waiter.
(8) One white apron for Bus Boy.
(9) Some tooth picks.
(10) One hat, badge and billy club for Constable.
(11) One large wallet.
(12) Two nightgowns.
(13) Two night caps.
(14) One whistle that Bus Boy uses to summon Constable.
(15) Two hand sticks with cut-out stars on them.
(16) Two hand sticks with cut-out moons on them.
(17) Two hand sticks with cut-out clouds on them.
(18) One long piece of colored yarn.
(19) Two handfuls of glitter.
(20) Two pairs of painter's overalls for Bags and Bags' dream person.

Production Notes:
The production of this story drama is one of the more elaborate in this book. Simplify it and adapt it in any way you wish to meet your needs.

The Tramps are all dressed poorly. Eustice I. Fleecem and

his dream figure are dressed similarly. The same is true of Bags and his dream figure.

At the beginning and end of dream sequences, the characters move to their places in slow motion.

Study Questions

(1) What do the characters in the parable symbolize or represent for you? Who is the Dives in you? Or, what part of you is like Dives? Who is the Lazarus in you? Who is the Abraham in you? Who is the dog in you? What is the abyss in you? How would you begin to bridge that abyss between you, Dives and Lazarus?

(2) Use some journal dialogue techniques with the different characters from this parable. In your journal write out your questions to the different characters as well as the replies that you imagine them to make to your questions. Another way to facilitate this dialogue is to get a partner and use a gestalt technique. Have two chairs. You sit in one and your partner in the other. Your partner is Dives. Ask Dives any questions you want. Your partner answers as Dives. Go for as long as you want. Now switch chairs. You are now Dives and your partner is the questioner. He or she may ask you any question now. Respond for/as your character. Try this with different characters in the parable. After completing the exercise, reflect on what you learned about your characters, your partner and yourself.

(3) What do the words "feasting" and "longing" mean to you? What do they evoke in you? Try a journal exercise that focuses on each of these words and experiences. Ask yourself the following questions: [1] What do I feast on? Or, what fills me? [2] What do I long for? Or, what am I hungry for? Ask each of these questions of yourself until you have no more responses. Don't move on to another question until you have exhausted the first for yourself.

(4) Joachim Jeremias contends that the parable of Dives and Lazarus is one of four double-edged parables: [1] Luke 15:11 and following [The Prodigal Child], [2] Luke 16:19–31 [Dives and Lazarus], [3] Matthew 20:1–16 [The Laborers in the Vineyard], and [4] Matthew 22:1–14 [The Wedding Banquet]. He contends that in all the double-edged parables the emphasis lies on the second point. In the parable of Dives and Lazarus, the first point is concerned with the reversal of fortune in the after-life. The second point has to do with Dives' five brothers. Experience this parable as one of the five brothers. Reflect on what you experience. Discuss.

(5) Lao-tzu said: "A journey of three thousand miles is begun by a single step." Imagine the steps that led Dives to the abode of the dead and the torment, and Lazarus to the joy of Abraham's bosom. Reflect on the steps of your own journey. Have they brought you fulfillment, frustration, or both? Can one change the direction of one's journey or life? How?

(6) What does Bags dream? What does Eustice dream? Do you think their dreams changed either of them? Why or why not? Do you remember any of your dreams? Do you believe in your dreams? Explain. John Sanford wrote a book entitled *Dreams: God's Forgotten Language*. Do you believe that God can speak to us through dreams? Why or why not? How can God speak to us through dreams? Can you remember any biblical stories about God speaking to people through dreams? Read Genesis 40:5–23, Genesis 41:1–43, 1 Kings 3:4–15, Matthew 1:18–25, Matthew 2:9–12, Matthew 2:13–15, and Matthew 2:19–23. During the next week try and remember your dreams. Write them down in your journal. Also write down what you think your dreams mean. Remember that every element in your dream is some part of you.

(7) This parable and this story drama deal with seeing, hearing, and acting. Take each of these verbs and work with it. Ask yourself three questions about each verb. [1] What does it mean to me to see, to hear, and to act? [2] What keeps or prevents me

from seeing, hearing and acting? [3] What are the steps I can and must take in order to see, to hear, and to act more?

(8) Both the parable and the story drama focus on food, those who have it in abundance, and those who don't have enough to survive. Have you ever been hungry? Have you ever gone to bed without something to eat? Have you ever fasted voluntarily, under the supervision of a spiritual director or medical doctor, as a religious practice? Did you know that fasting has a long tradition in the history of Christianity and other world religions? Do some study and reading on fasting. Why do people fast? For most of us, fasting is a periodic choice and not a way of life. Do you know anything about world hunger? Write to *Bread for the World* [32 Union Square East/New York, New York 10003] or some other national organization that works with world hunger and ask them to send you any information that they can.

Bibliography

Brueggemann, Walter. *The Prophetic Imagination.* Philadelphia: Fortress Press, 1978.

Brown, Raymond E. *et al.,* eds. *The Jerome Biblical Commentary.* Englewood Cliffs, N.J.: Prentice-Hall, Inc., 1968.

Buechner, Frederick. *Telling the Truth: The Gospel as Tragedy, Comedy, and Fairy Tale.* New York: Harper and Row, 1977.

Crossan, John Dominic. *In Parables: The Challenge of the Historical Jesus.* New York: Harper and Row, 1973.

———. *The Dark Interval: Towards a Theology of Story.* Niles, Ill.: Argus Communications, 1975.

———. *Clifts of Fall: Paradox and Polyvalence in the Parables of Jesus.* New York: The Seabury Press, 1980.

Dodd, C. H. *The Parables of the Kingdom.* New York: Charles Scribner's Sons, 1961.

Donahue, John R. "Bridging the Gap." *Liturgical Prayer* 3 (February 1973):3.

———. "Miracle, Mystery and Parable." *Way* 18 (October 1978):260.

Empereur, James L. Foreword to *How the Word Became Flesh: Story Dramas for Education and Worship,* by Michael E. Moynahan. Saratoga, Cal.: Resource Publications, 1981.

Funk, Robert. *Language, Hermeneutic and Word of God.* New York: Harper and Row, 1966.

Holmes, Urban T., III. *Ministry and Imagination.* New York: The Seabury Press, 1976.

Hopkins, Gerard Manley. *The Poems of Gerard Manley Hopkins.* Edited by W. H. Gardner and N. H. Mackenzie. London: Oxford University Press, 1967.

Howes, Elizabeth Boyden. *Intersection and Beyond.* San Francisco: Guild for Psychological Studies, 1971.

————, and Moon, Sheila. *The Choicemaker.* Philadelphia: The Westminster Press, 1973.

Jeremias, Joachim. *The Parables of Jesus.* New York: Charles Scribner's Sons, 1963.

Laymon, Charles M., ed. *The Interpreter's One-Volume Commentary on the Bible.* Nashville: Abingdon Press, 1971.

Lynch, William. *Images of Hope.* Notre Dame: University of Notre Dame Press, 1965.

————. *Images of Faith.* Notre Dame: University of Notre Dame Press, 1973.

McFague, Sallie. *Speaking in Parables.* Philadelphia: Fortress Press, 1975.

Moynahan, Michael. *How the Word Became Flesh: Story Dramas for Worship and Religious Education.* Saratoga, Cal.: Resource Publications, 1981.

Newman, Louis I., ed. *Hasidic Anthology.* New York: Shocken Books, 1963.

Nouwen, Henri J. M. *Creative Ministry.* Garden City, N.Y.: Doubleday and Company, Inc., 1971.

Ochs, Robert. *God Is More Present Than You Think.* New York: Paulist Press, 1970.

Palmer, Richard E. *Hermeneutics.* Evanston: Northwestern University Press, 1969.

Perkins, Pheme. *Hearing the Parables of Jesus.* New York: Paulist Press, 1981.

Perrin, Norman. *Rediscovering the Teaching of Jesus.* New York: Harper and Row, 1976.

————. *Jesus and the Language of the Kingdom.* Philadelphia: Fortress Press, 1976.

Polanyi, Michael, and Prosch, Harry. *Meaning.* Chicago: The University of Chicago Press, 1975.

Ricoeur, Paul. *The Philosophy of Paul Ricoeur.* Edited by Charles E. Reagan and David Stewart. Boston: Beacon Press, 1978.

Sanford, John A. *The Kingdom Within.* Philadelphia: J. B. Lippincott Company, 1970.

Shea, John. *Stories of God.* Chicago: The Thomas More Press, 1978.

————. *Stories of Faith.* Chicago: The Thomas More Press, 1980.

Throckmorton, Burton H., ed. *Gospel Parallels.* Toronto: Thomas Nelson and Sons, 1949.

Tolbert, Mary Ann. *Perspectives on the Parables: An Approach to Multiple Interpretations.* Philadelphia: Fortress Press, 1979.

Tracy, David. *Blessed Rage for Order.* New York: The Seabury Press, 1978.

Via, Dan Otto, Jr. *The Parables.* Philadelphia: Fortress Press, 1967.

Westerhoff, John H., III. *Will Our Children Have Faith?* New York: The Seabury Press, 1976.

Wheelwright, Philip. *Metaphor and Reality.* Bloomington: University of Indiana Press, 1962.

White, James F. *New Forms of Worship.* New York: Abingdon Press, 1971.

————. *Introduction to Christian Worship.* Nashville: Abingdon Press, 1980.

Wilder, Amos N. *Early Christian Rhetoric.* Cambridge: Harvard University Press, 1978.

————. *Theopoetic: Theology and the Religious Imagination.* Philadelphia: Fortress Press, 1976.

Wink, Walter. *The Bible in Human Transformation.* Philadelphia: Fortress Press, 1973.

————. *Transforming Bible Study.* Nashville: Abingdon Press, 1980.

Young, Robert D. *Religious Imagination: God's Gift to Prophets and Preachers.* Philadelphia: The Westminster Press, 1970.

Zimmer, Heinrich. *The King and the Corpse.* Edited by Joseph Campbell. Princeton: Princeton University Press, 1957.

Additional Materials Used:

M. Boucher, *The Parables, New Testament Message* # 7 (Wilmington, Delaware: Michael Glazier, 1981.)

J. Breech, *The Silence of Jesus: The Authentic Voice of the Historical Man* (Philadelphia: Fortress Press, 1983.)

J. Lambrecht, *Once More Astonished: The Parables of Jesus* (New York: Crossroads, 1982.)